A PRACTICAL STEP·BY·STEP GUIDE TO

BONSAI

FOR THE HOME AND GARDEN

A PRACTICAL STEP·BY·STEP GUIDE TO

BONSAI

FOR THE HOME AND GARDEN

LEONARD WEBBER

ANGUS
& ROBERTSON
PUBLISHERS

ANGUS & ROBERTSON PUBLISHERS

Unit 4, Eden Park, 31 Waterloo Road,
North Ryde, NSW, Australia 2113, and
16 Golden Square, London WIR 4BN,
United Kingdom.

First published in Australia
by Angus & Robertson Publishers in 1985
First published in the United Kingdom
by Angus & Robertson (UK) in 1986
Reprinted 1986, 1987, 1988, 1989

National Library of Australia
Cataloguing-in-publication data.

Webber, Leonard.
  Bonsai for the home and garden.

  ISBN 0 207 15018 4.

  1. Bonsai, 1. Title.

635.9'772

Typeset in 10/11 pt Tiffany medium
by Setrite Typesetters, Hong Kong
Printed in Italy

CONTENTS

BONSAI – THE BEGINNINGS

Bonsai 1. The art of growing dwarfed ornamental varieties
of trees or shrubs in small shallow pots by selective pruning.
2. A tree or shrub grown by this method.

Collins English Dictionary

The word bonsai, pronounced bon-sigh, is made up of two characters: *bon* meaning "tray" or "pot", and *sai*, to plant. The sound of the word is Japanese but the characters for it are Chinese and, indeed, such a mixed derivation is appropriate. This extraordinary branch of horticulture was originated by the Chinese and later refined by the Japanese who were responsible for its introduction to the western world.

Bonsai is one of the most exciting forms of horticulture ever to be practised. Giant trees can be reduced to proportions so small that they may be held in the palm of the hand. Many hundreds of years of highly skilled horticultural techniques have given rise to these tree replicas, designed and cared for in shallow containers sometimes containing less than a tablespoonful of soil.

The first hint of the art is a legend dating back to the Han period of dynastic rule in China between 206 BC and 220 AD over 2000 years ago. According to the legend, Fei Jiang Feng of the Han dynasty possessed the magic power of "shrinking the earth" by dwarfing mountains and rivers, trees, birds and beasts, houses, boats, carriages and human beings, which he then put inside a small urn. While Feng's influence over land forms, fauna and transport are, of course, mythical, it is nevertheless believed that he was a dwarf-tree fancier who "brought landscapes indoors".

By the time of the T'sin dynasty, 265-420, the art of bonsai, or *penjing* as it is known in China, was being described in literary writings, and mentions continue to be found in the writings of the Tang dynasty, 618-906. What are believed to be the earliest pictorial records of penjing/bonsai also date from this dynastic period and show that bonsai was an art form appreciated in the imperial court more than 1200 years ago.

In 1972 Chinese archaeologists unearthed an ancient tomb in Shaanxi Province. Built in 706 AD, it contained the remains of Prince Zhang Huai, the second son of Empress Wu Zetian of the Tang dynasty. The murals on the walls of the tomb depict court life. Two of these, to the surprise of horticulturalists, show ladies-in-waiting in court attire holding potted landscapes with miniature rockeries and fruit trees.

While bonsai is believed to have reached Japan almost 1000 years ago, its oldest records date from the beginning of the thirteenth century, but these show it as a highly disciplined art. The records are found in scrolls which illustrate the miraculous effect of prayers offered at the Kasuga Shrine in Nara and the principal events in the life of the priest Honen Shonin (1133-1212), the founder of the Jodo sect of Buddhism. In one scroll particularly, the *Tsurezure Gusa* by Kenko Yoshida, it seems apparent that Honen Shonin was an enthusiastic practitioner of bonsai.

Here we see pictures of trees or grasses transplanted from the outdoors in shallow pots as garden ornaments. This way of admiring plants in those far-off days, despite the fact that planting flowers and trees in a garden had already become a custom, shows the appreciation of the beautiful as expressed in the form of bonsai. A century later Kasugagongin's historical picture scrolled by Takakane Takoshima, dated 1309, also depicts bonsai.

Then in the fifteenth century, which is known as the Nuromachi period in Japanese history, there is found another reference to bonsai in the famous Noh play entitled *Hachi-no-Ki*, or *The Potted Trees*. The play uses the fact that in those days the people loved to cultivate in pots such trees as the pine, the Japanese apricot and the cherry. In this play a penniless but nevertheless warm-hearted and faithful samurai, Sano Genzaemon, makes fuel of his favourite potted pine to warm his guest who proves to be a shogun travelling incognito.

Bonsai became very popular in Japan with all classes, aristocrats and peasants taking a great interest in growing them. At the beginning of the Meiji period of Japanese history in 1869, the name bonsai was officially proclaimed by sponsors and was adopted throughout Japan.

After an exhibition in 1934 in the Ueno Park Art Gallery, bonsai was recognised as a work of art and was given a competitive position with other nationally known objects of beauty. Since then it has become very popular as one of the most honoured arts and has been respected as such even by the uninitiated.

The Ueno exhibitions — there was one in spring and one in autumn that first year — known as the Kokufu Bonsai Exhibitions, became annual events; they were suspended by the outbreak of the Pacific war but resumed in 1947.

Until the turn of the century, bonsai had never been seen in any quantity outside Japan and their first appearance at an exhibition in London in 1909 created a sensation and some demand for the plants. I have in my possession a descriptive catalogue of bulbs, plants and seeds from the Yokohama Nursery Co. Ltd, dated 1911-12. The word bonsai is not mentioned and the section dealing with miniature trees is headed "Dwarfed Trees growing in Jardiniers". A list of names is included of those plants available, from $1 to $50, prices being in American gold. An American gold dollar is stated as equivalent to four shillings, four marks or five francs. It also adds that mails from Europe should be marked "Via Siberia" on the envelope as ". . . it will reach here in three weeks or so, otherwise it will take over 50 days". The price for a 10-year-old Chinese elm, *Ulmus parvifolia*, three-quarters of an inch (2 cm) in diameter, is US $3.05. A 10-year-old Chinese juniper, *Juniperus chinensis*, growing on a rock

(with pumice stone) is US $25. The Trident maple, *Acer buergeranum*, seven to eight years old, is a mere US $1.11!

As the trees on twice-annual exhibition in Ueno Park grew more beautiful every year, so too did the popularity of bonsai grow. People from various parts of the world went to Japan to learn the art and to unravel its secrets, so that eventually one of the national arts of Japan became an international art of the world.

What is it that attracts so many? Perhaps it is the ability to shape nature so demonstrably or maybe it is the fascination of the seemingly impossible — a plant's longevity under such apparently inhospitable conditions.

With respect to the latter, I am reminded of one old bonsai that came into my care. It was an ancient Chinese banyan brought into Australia in the mid-nineteen twenties by an old sea-captain. The tree was exciting to look at: it was shaped like a human body, with two roots exposed above soil level as the top of the legs, two branches shaped and trained upwards as the arms and with five small branches as fingers. But most of these were dead. At the top of the trunk where the arms took their rise was a porcelain head of Chinese origin which completed the work of art.

It must have been over 100 years old when I first sighted it and had for several decades been used as a "doorstop" for a front door. When the door was open, the bonsai was moved by the foot and guided into place to stop the door closing. In all this time the banyan had had no treatment at all and was in a bad state, the soil much like dust. Yet, after all this time, when it was repotted in a slightly larger pot vigorous growth occurred and I was able to prune it in an effort to force out new branches lower down so that the "finger" branches could be encouraged and re-established.

The idea of age with smallness is facinating but as Yuji Yoshimura, author of *The Japanese Art of Miniature Trees and Landscapes*, warns, it has "led many wes-

Top and Bottom: In these rock settings from Omiya Nursery, Japan,
the rock in effect serves instead of a pot.
The settings themselves suggest distant mountain scenes.

Top: View of a bonsai nursery in Omiya.
Bottom: *Zelkova serrata* is the traditional Japanese choice
for the broom style bonsai.

n people to give undue importance to
e age of the tree. They tend to expect a
nsai to be hundreds of years old and are
sappointed to learn that it is not. They
rget that the most important thing about
bonsai is its beauty." Bonsai are for
oking at with pleasure and, from their
ginnings, this always has been their
le. In tracing the origins of the art, it is
w believed that it stems from an ap-
eciation of flowers — the Chinese
stom of introducing small flowering
ricot trees into their homes in cel-
ration of the spring that was soon to
llow.

The apricot is the first of the spring
owering trees to produce blossom and
ore likely to flower in late winter than
ring. Because of its early flowering, it
s grown in pots so that it could be
ought into the house and admired at that
ne of the year when other flowers were
n-existent.

Apricot blossom was considered to
the harbinger of spring and became
rt of the religious ceremonies and
uals, a sort of thanksgiving that the
eak winter season was approaching its
d. It would appear that the trees were
uned and repotted to give abundant
wer and a longer life, eventually being
aped by the persistent pruning and
ing trained into attractive shapes.

It is in the spirit of those early
inese gardeners who made it possible to
ng spring inside that *Bonsai for the
me and Garden* is written.

The Chinese were the originators of the horticultural art of bonsai, or *penjing* as it is known in China. This early Chinese painting shows three specimens.

The Japanese refined the art, setting up the various style classifications and techniques that are followed today. Below are two early prints in which bonsai specimens feature.

AN APPRECIATION OF TREES

In the early stages of bonsai study, very few students really understand tree shapes. In most western countries, tree shapes are judged by the mature shape of the head of the tree. Such terminology as "half-rounded head", "dense rounded head", "erect main branches", and "tree-like habit with spreading branches" are commonly used to describe trees, and no reference whatever is made to the shape of the trunk.

Japan is the only country in the world that has classified its trees according to the shape of the trunk. In bonsai culture, these shapes are the future styles to which a tree is trained. It therefore becomes important that bonsai growers not only study horticultural techniques, but also take time to study living trees. Make a visit to the nearest botanical gardens, or even a walk in a garden suburb, and make a point of examining the individual characteristics of the trees and shrubs. For example, look closely at the shape of the trunk, bark colour and texture, arrangement of the branches, foliage size and colour, and details of leaf shape, flower and fruit. Look especially at the base of the tree for the emergence of the roots radiating from the trunk at soil level. There is immense variety. Trees with two trunks, trees with many trunks, upright trees, informal trees, slanting trees, straight branches, crooked branches, evergreen trees, deciduous trees, and trees with bare roots leaving the protection of the soil to creep over rocks, following the contours of crevices and returning to the soil at the bottom of the rock.

These are the details that the bonsai grower should look for to apply to his or her own trees.

Appreciating Bonsai

The Japanese have a saying: "First the trunk, second the branches, and third the roots." Not only is this the sequence of events in training the tree, but it is also the order of importance attached to the va[ri]ous parts of the tree as bonsai specimen[s].

Trunk
The trunk should not have any scars [or] imperfections. It should taper natura[lly] from the base to the top. Trees severe[ly] pruned to drastically reduce the heig[ht] lack this quality and may be frowned up[on] by the purists. Some exaggeration is ine[vi]table, but the scars can be concealed [by] the future growth of branches and leav[es].

Branches
The branches form the framework of t[he] tree. Their length, shape and dispositi[on] are usually governed by fairly strict rule[s]. Expert opinion differs and some say th[at] the branches should follow the law [of] naturalness and should not be tied do[wn] by strict rules. For example, a Japane[se] maple with formal rigid branches, neat[ly] pruned, looks artificial compared with o[ne] that has branches with pendulous ti[ps] which, when in leaf, almost conceal t[he] skeleton of trunk and branch. Regardle[ss] of the style, the rules say that the branch[es] should be arranged in an alternate mann[er] — that is, they leave the trunk first fro[m] one side then from another higher up. It [is] the pruning of the branches to vario[us] style criteria that determines a good [or] bad bonsai. The word that best express[es] the relationship between the trunk a[nd] branches is harmony.

Leaves
Some trees bear leaves which wi[ll] without any inducement, reduce their si[ze] in proportion to the size of the trun[k]. Other trees have large leaves which c[an] cause consternation among bonsai growe[rs] who concentrate on the smaller sizes [of] bonsai. Examples of trees with sm[all] leaves and some of those which redu[ce] leaf size will be found in the select list [of] plant material on page 65.

Shape, colour and texture of leav[es] may be the factors that determine t[he] selection of a tree. Some are chosen f[or] the pastel greens of their new leave[s]

everal species of maple are particularly
opular for this reason. At the other
xtreme, it is the gorgeous colour of
utumn foliage that attracts attention.
yssa sylvatica and *Liquidambar styraciflua*
re good examples. The texture of the leaf
ay be the determining factor, from the
oft, delicate look of the Japanese maple,
cer palmatum, to the glossy hard surface
f the genus *Camellia*. Shape is as variable
s the plants themselves. The needle-like
aves of the pines, the divided (lobed)
aves of the maples, the scale-like leaves
f the junipers, the sharp, toothed margin
f the flowering cherry, and the compound
af of the wisteria all have their charm
nd attraction.

Roots

The final touch in designing the bonsai is
to have an attractive root system visible at
soil level. It should be arranged in a natural
radiating pattern. It must give the appearance that the root system has a good grip
on the earth and, at the same time, a look
of maturity, typical of the aged trees in
parks and the natural landscape. Defects
in the root system are hard to overcome.
Care must be taken in the early stages of
training to arrange the roots for later
exposure when the bonsai is presented in
the ornamental pot.

If there are any secrets in bonsai
culture, they exist here in an appreciation
of the design of trees.

single Japanese maple has been trained to produce
ree trunks which give the appearance of a natural
ump of individual trees.

CLASSIFICATION OF BONSAI
FIRST THE TRUNK

Size, shape, habit of growth, group-ings and settings are all considered and represented in traditional Japanese classification of bonsai.

Size

There are four groups in the classification for size. The Japanese display some reluc-tance to set precise size limitations within each category, believing that the limi-tations are arrived at by individual good taste. While it is good to have some freedom of movement in deciding the ultimate height of your own miniature trees, the following approximations may prove helpful.

Miniature
These are the midget bonsai ranging from about 5 cm up to a maximum of about 18 cm. Minimum size once again is related to good taste and there is no prize for produc-ing the smallest. A useful guideline to size is that a number of trees of these dimen-sions may be safely held on one hand. Those that qualify as *shito bonsai* are usually referred to as fingertip bonsai, that is, the tree and its pot may be held on the tip of the finger.

Perhaps surprisingly, selection of plant material for this work is unlimited. There is no restriction placed on the use of natural dwarf and slow-growing forms. Flowering and fruiting trees, especially those with miniature flowers and fruits, are extremely popular in Japan, as well as the maples and pines. Regardless of their size, miniature bonsai perform all the normal botanical functions of their bigger counterparts. They grow, they flower and they produce fruit.

Small
The second stage of bonsai reaches a height of approximately 30 cm. A very attractive-looking tree can be designed within this limitation.

Medium
This is perhaps the most popular size in Japan. The ultimate is a beautifully propor-

tioned tree, not too cumbersome to handl and train, not too heavy to lift and shift and reaching its peak at about 65 cm.

Large
The limitations on big bonsai are perhap more vague than any other category ranging from 65 cm to 100 cm or more This size gives almost complete freedom to select something compatible with th grower's own capacity to shape and train and, more important, handle the large tre with its container and volume of soil Those who wish to grow large bonsai, take heart. Some of the big trees in Japan are further classified as "two-man trees" o "three-man trees". The inference is that i takes two or more people to lift and shift

Shape

As mentioned earlier, Japan is the onl country in the world that classifies a tre according to the shape of the trunk. It i this classification which is responsible fo the ultimate shape of bonsai.

Not all trees grow straight upwards Some have a natural curve; some are shaped by wind or their struggle to reacl sunlight. It is these differences found i nature that are reproduced by craft i bonsai.

Formal Upright Style
The word "formal" is the descriptive word suggesting a tree with a clean, straigh trunk, free from scars and imperfections and tapering from the widest part of th trunk at soil level. The branches radiat from the trunk at right angles, the larges towards the bottom. From the bottom branch to the apex should be about two thirds the total length of the tree. This would mean that the lowest branch would be about one-third up from soil level.

Even these rules are often disre garded. The highly skilled bonsai maste may even arrange the branches almos from soil level. Japanese pictorial bonsa books can be very rewarding whe studying this classification. Here it is seer

hat the branches are arranged alter-
ately. The lowest branch may be on the
ight-hand side of the tree, the next one on
ie left, and in between these two is the
ack branch. In the perfect tree, this
rrangement continues to the top of the
runk, thus giving the effect of branches
adiating from bottom to top in all
irections.

To stop the branches growing into
ach other, they are pruned and shaped,
rstly in a flat horizontal arrangement
hich keeps them separated in the hori-
ontal plane. Secondly, pruning controls
ie length of the main branch and its
ffshooting branchlets. To control the
eight of the tree, the leader or central
tem is persistently pruned, and as the
ee matures it may require only the new

buds to be nipped out on the top. The
proportion of the branches to each other
and to the general size of the tree, and the
spacing of the branches along the length of
the trunk, are not precisely measured. The
proportion is a visual one. The bonsai
grower tries to create a beautiful living
tree with a pleasing visual impact. Any
tree with a naturally upright habit of
growth is suitable for this style. In Japan
the most popular species used are the five-
needle pine, black pine and, less often,
Cryptomeria japonica; but Japanese maple,
usually seen as an informal tree, can also
be trained as a formal upright.

Traditionally formal upright style
trees are placed only in rectangular pots.

Informal Upright Style
Trees that have a natural curved trunk or
stem, such as jacaranda or cotoneaster
and vines like wisteria, are the inspiration
for this style. It is sometimes referred to as
the curved trunk style. Its basic direction
is upwards but it is irregular in its movement. The final shape should be informal
but well balanced. If the trunk is straight,
the branches are straight; if the trunk is
irregular, so are the branches. The arrangement of the branches follows closely
the alternating pattern of the formal upright style except that the origin of the
branch should be on the outside of a curve.
This can restrict the total number of
branches but the different shapes to which
the trunk can be designed are numerous.
In fact it would be difficult to find two
identically styled trees in any collection or
at any exhibition.

Good taste dictates the number of
curves in the trunk. Two or three are
usually adequate in its total length and
more than this is considered monotonous.
Trees designed in a series of bends or
curves are designated "octopus style", but
the style is no longer popular.

The informal nature of this style
does not necessarily mean that curves are
essential. The trunk may be reasonably
straight but planted slightly away from the
vertical plane at an angle of about 11
degrees. If the slant is greater than this, it

ORMAL UPRIGHT STYLE
Jsually described as a "straight trunk",
he trunk itself must be free from scars
nd imperfections, tapering from the base
o the top, the branches arranged
lternately.

could be confused with the slanting trunk style (see below).

In the final design the top of the tree is bent slightly forward towards the front of the tree, and the top of the trunk is directly in line with the centre of the base. The reduction in the number of branches compared with the formal upright style should make it an easier tree to train and this may be a factor in its popularity.

This is a style that is suitable for a large range of trees. Fruiting and flowering trees, evergreens like conifers and figs and deciduous trees like maples, elms, oaks and ashes, all can be trained in the informal upright shape.

Round-, oval-, rectangular, octagonal- and hexagonal-shaped pots are all suitable for this bonsai style.

Slanting-trunk Style

Although on first encounter this may seem a somewhat contrived style, the inspiration for this, as with all bonsai styles, comes from growth patterns observed in nature.

A young tree where the root system has yet to perform the function of anchorage may be blown away from the vertical line by a strong wind or storm and may continue to grow in a slanting direction. Or a tree on a slope will often be observed growing more or less at right angles to the slope. As another example, trees planted close together may force one or more in a slanting direction in an effort to seek light or sunshine. These are popularly assumed to be the original inspirations for this style. While not very common, designing a tree to replicate this shape offers a challenge to the bonsai grower.

The branch arrangement of this style is somewhat different from an upright tree. As in nature, the most prolific growth will occur on the sunny or upper side of the trunk, very often giving a one-sided tree, since the density of the prolific growth on the upper side casts a shadow which deprives the under-branches of light, in turn killing the foliage. The angle

INFORMAL UPRIGHT STYLE
The irregular shape and curved trunk make this a popular subject. The informal style allows a tremendous range of tree designs.

SLANTING-TRUNK STYLE
The variation in the individual trees and the interpretation of the slanting trunk produce almost as many different shapes as the informal style.

the slant may vary from slightly more
an 11 degrees from the vertical to
most approaching horizontal, but the top
the tree always turns upwards.

This style may be achieved by the
se of wire or by planting the tree at an
ngle.

Mountain tree species are most often
ained in this style, thus most of the
onifers are suitable. Most pot shapes can
e used; with rectangular or oval pots, if a
ee is positioned to the left of the pot, it
ould be slanted to the right and *vice
ersa*.

emi-cascade Style

ght and shade plus environment can
oduce natural horizontal growth pat-
rns. For example, trees growing on rocks
vertical rock surfaces often assume this
ape. The trunk grows out in a horizontal
rection and all the branches arise from
e upper side of the trunk in a very un-
sual pattern. Such a pattern of growth is
ormalised in the semi-cascade and cas-
de style of bonsai. The branches are
ained to produce a tree-like shape on the
pper side of the trunk.

This style of bonsai is usually grown
a tall pot to counterbalance the weight
the extended trunk and branches. The

weight of the pot and the greater volume
of soil are also needed as anchorage to
stop the tree pulling out of the pot or
upsetting it.

On rare occasions, one may come
across an unusual tree ideally suited to
this style. Two ideal forms are a horizontal form of the Japanese maple, *Acer
palmatum* "Horizontalis", and a horizontally growing English hawthorn, *Crataegus
laevigata* "Horizontalis". The latter is a
superior flowering and fruiting hawthorn.
But there are few restrictions, if any, in
the selection of plant material for the semi-
cascade style. The Japanese are particularly fond of shaping chrysanthemums in
this and the cascade style and the sight of
massed pots at chrysanthemum shows is
extremely beautiful.

Semi-cascade trees are presented in
deep pots which are available in round,
square and many-sided shapes.

Cascade Style

The trunk of the tree emerging from the

CASCADE
A tree growing 180 degrees from the
normal upright position is reasonably
common in nature, especially in moun-
tainous areas. A very graceful design can
be induced in this style. The length of the
fall may be to the bottom of the pot or
extending 1 m or more.

EMI-CASCADE STYLE
sually depicted as a tree growing in
horizontal position, there are many
ariations.

soil is upright. It then turns abruptly at 180 degrees to grow downwards. The length of the fall may vary from tree to tree and according to personal taste. It is classified as cascade once the tip of the cascading trunk grows below the level of the rim of the pot. However, it should be realised that trees that are normally vigorous upright growers should not be trained into this style. Like the semi-cascade style, tall pots are used for planting and this style is best displayed placed on a table or tall stand which accentuates the cascading trunk.

While conifers are very popular subjects for training in this style, naturally informal trees and shrubs like jacaranda, azalea and dogwood can be trained, and those having natural weeping habits like *Cotoneaster horizontalis* and willow are used, together with the climbing vines, which, if having nothing to climb upon, will weep naturally. Wisteria is a particular favourite in Japan.

Number of Trees in a Pot

Bonsai classification also embraces gro plantings where two or more trees the same species or cultivar are plant together in one pot. Only on very r occasions would two different species planted together.

There is little restriction on pla material. Most popular species are su able for this style, including mapl conifers and even flowering shrubs l azaleas.

Two Trees

In a two-tree planting, one tree, oft referred to as the mother tree, domina the setting with the second smaller tr subordinate to it. They are usually plant close together with the second tree plac slightly to the front or rear of the moth tree. Two trees are never planted in li with each other, parallel to the front ed of the pot.

The Japanese maple is an excelle

A two-tree setting of a trident maple.

species to work with in this style. Pot shapes are unrestricted.

Groups Proper

These consist of an assembly of trees traditionally made up of an odd number: three, five, seven or nine. Where more than nine trees are to be planted together, the name *multiple trees* is applied. The arrangement of the trees within the group — that is, the spacing between the trees and the relationships of the trees to each other — can vary and can be further classified as a *cluster group* or a *natural*

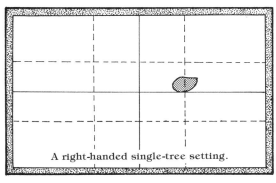

A right-handed single-tree setting.

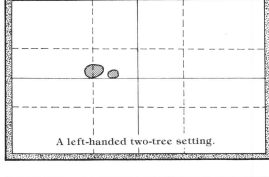

A left-handed two-tree setting.

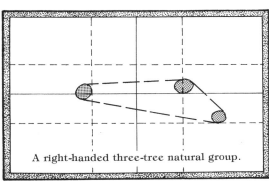

A right-handed three-tree natural group.

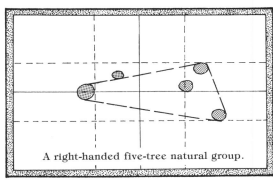

A right-handed five-tree natural group.

POSITIONING A SINGLE TREE AND NATURAL GROUPS

In round, square, many-sided and petal pots, natural groupings are planted so that the centre of the pot is the symmetrical centre of the group. A single tree is planted as accurately as possible in the centre of the pot.

In rectangular or oval pots, placement of trees is always asymmetric. As a positioning guide, imagine the pot is quartered (solid lines) then divided into thirds (dotted lines). The single or major tree is always positioned one-third in from the end and slightly behind the halfway mark of the pot on either the right-hand side, as shown, or the left. Three-tree and five-tree settings could be positioned as shown.

POSITIONING TWO-TREE OR TWIN-TRUNK SETTINGS

In two-tree or twin-trunk settings, a rectangular or oval pot is generally used. As a positioning guide, imagine the pot is halved (solid line) then divided into thirds (dotted lines). The larger trunk is positioned as shown with the subordinate tree placed slightly to the front *or* rear of the mother tree.

group. In a cluster group, trees are planted close together in a circular cluster. A natural group, as its name suggests, is a group of trees seeming to be naturally spaced. In fact the spacing of natural groups follows fairly formal positioning with the major tree being positioned carefully one-third from the end of the pot and just behind the halfway line taken from front to back (see diagrams).

Multiple Trunks

Encountered within this classification are those settings that appear to be groups of trees but which, when carefully examined, are seen to be trunks joined together and having a common root system.

Twin trunk, the first of these styles, has for its counterpart the two-tree setting of the group plantings. Its general appearance is very similar except that the origin of the second trunk, that is, where it is joined to the mother trunk, is visible above soil level. On some occasions, the second trunk may rise above soil level and look like a branch rather than a trunk.

Trees with three trunks and five trunks may be observed by the keen student in the local environment; but in bonsai, multiple trunk styles are much sought after because of their rarity. Two very popular multiple trunk styles are the clump style and the raft style.

The clump style mimics those trees and shrubs which produce a series of shoots around their base and its counterpart is the cluster group setting.

Raft style is one of the most popular bonsai styles and duplicates a tree which has been blown down yet survives to grow new shoots which become future trees. There are two types of raft style — the straight and the sinuous. The latter, somewhat resembling a natural setting, is simply an informal-upright-shaped tree, prostrate on the ground.

Maples, crabapples, cherries, figs and most conifers can be trained in these multiple trunk styles, which are usually presented in pots that conform to the shape of the setting. Twin-tree and clump-style settings would be presented in pots that are roundish in shape while the raft style is usually presented in oblong or rectangular containers.

Trees Growing on a Rock

Trees growing on rocks are commonplace in nature. The Japanese have studied this very carefully, noting not only the particular beauty in the combination of plant and rock, but also the different habits of growth. In his work *The Japanese Art of Miniature Trees and Landscapes*, Yoshimura classifies the rock settings under two headings: "root over rock" and "clinging to a rock".

Fig, root over rock style.

Root over Rock

The tree or plant in this style of bonsai grows on a rock which stands on a bed of soil. The plant's roots are trained over the rock and down into the soil. This type of tree is often seen in nature, particularly in rugged mountain areas or where exposed rocks are abundant. In the Royal Botanic Gardens in Sydney, for example, fig trees can be seen growing on an elevated rock shelf. The root system leaves the protection of the soil and creeps over the rocks, conforming to the rock's contours; the roots then re-enter the soil lower down. Some roots may enter rock crevices or follow the line of the crevice, then move ownwards towards the lower soil level. The term root over rock is an apt description. John Naka, author of *Bonsai Techniques*, gives Japanese terminology. He ses the word *ishusuke* to describe a plant owing this way. This style is usually nited to a single tree or a small group of e same species.

Because of its splendid root system, e trident maple is often used in this etting, but all trees with vigorous root stems are suitable. These include figs, ack pine or, indeed, most other pines, d azaleas. Pots for this setting are additionally very shallow and, depending the size of the rock, would seldom be ore than 5 cm deep.

g, clinging to a rock style.

linging to a Rock
he difference in this style of bonsai is at the tree exists on the rock with its own upply of soil and therefore becomes an dependent living plant. The rock in ffect serves instead of a pot and this type f setting is usually displayed in an rnamental shallow tray with no drainage les, called a *suiban*.

John Naka's terminology for this yle is *ishi-uye*. Traditionally, the trees sed in this type of setting are those where e natural habitat is a mountain environ-ent, so that the setting itself suggests a

distant mountain scene. The pines, spruces, junipers and mountain maple are thus commonly used. On occasions, the tiny-flowered species of azalea are planted near the base of the rock, giving a beautiful contrast in the spring.

This classification allows for a number of different species to be used. It is the only classification that traditionally allows for mixed plantings. This requires much more skill to assemble and more care and maintenance to keep in good condition. Thus it may be prudent to study and select those trees which show tolerance to dry conditions.

Other Popular Bonsai Styles

It is generally accepted that the shape of bonsai is taken from the shapes of trees growing naturally. As these appear to be almost unlimited in design, it will come as no surprise to learn that there is an abundance of bonsai styles — too many to cover usefully in a work such as this. However, the following are popular and often seen in exhibitions or publications.

Octopus Style
A tree with many curves and often many branches starting from soil level represents this style. The many legs of the octopus is the unusual basis for the style. In a recent Japanese publication it was recorded as "no longer popular".

Broom Style
A tree with regular, almost vertical branching would be the ideal tree to use. *Zelkova serrata* is the traditional Japanese choice and sometimes the related trees, the elms, are used. The trunk is usually reduced in height and new branches arising mostly in close proximity are all trained. One branch is selected as a leader and trained vertically, while the others are angled slightly on both sides, the result resembling the old-fashioned broom where twigs of the branch were bundled and tied onto the broom handle.

Windswept Style
Trees exposed to prevailing winds produce this style in nature. Copper wire and pruning give the same results in bonsai.

Coiled Style
In this style the trunk has a coil of about 360 degrees, either in the vertical or horizontal plane, which is produced by wiring and may require four to five years or more to perfect.

Weeping-branch Style
This is the counterpart of the garde weeping tree. The first time I saw this Japan it was restricted to the weepi apricot. Most of the weeping or horizont; growing trees can be used for this sty and they can be either grown from cuttin and trained or, for quicker results, graft onto a formal or informal trunk or even semi-cascade trunk. The weeping branch are trained by wire.

English hawthorn, coiled style.

Twisted-trunk Style
In this style it appears that the trunk has been physically twisted, but this is an illusion achieved by horticultural sleight of hand. A spiral strip of bark is carefully removed from the trunk. When the tissue beneath heals, it leaves a conspicuous spiral scar which gives the appearance of a twist.

Driftwood Style
This style presents another damaged tree. Here emphasis is placed on the scrubbing and bleaching of the damaged parts, so they look like the smooth white surface of driftwood.

Sasanqua camellia, weeping-branch style.

plit-trunk Style

any of these are developed from old
tural trees which have suffered some
mage, such as being hit by lightning. In
 simple form, a severe wound is visible
here it appears that a large portion of the
rk has been peeled off and, indeed, this
 how the style is created.

Bunjin or literati style

Exposed-root Style

Flood waters, typhoons and storms all
remove the soil in large quantities, leaving
trees standing with their major roots
exposed. Such trees are the inspiration for
this style. Trees with a known vigorous or
showy root system are used for this style,
since the roots play a major part in the
display. Trees can be grown in deep containers to achieve necessary root length.

g, split-trunk style.

unjin or Literati Style

his style is distinguished by the presen-
tion of a slender trunk, often of unusual
esign and with few branches. Its posture
n range from upright to cascade, so it is
nsidered to be free form. Having less
straints than other styles, it is extremely
pular and readily achieved by pruning
d wiring.

Trident maple, exposed-root style.

TRAINING FOR SIZE, SHAPE AND SETTING
SECOND THE BRANCHES

Pruning and wiring are probably of equal importance in training bonsai, since the tree is controlled by pruning and wiring its shape induced by the aid of copper wire.

Wiring

There are very few informal bonsai styles achieved without the aid of wire. The graceful curve of the informal trunk, the shaping and positioning of the branches to match the trunk, and the sweeping curve of the cascade would be difficult indeed to produce.

Supple and Rigid Wood
The individual grower must be able appreciate the different tensile strength of the wood in the trees selected f bonsai.

The home handyman or woman probably already aware of such terms hardwood and softwood as applied timber. The same classification could used for living trees, but the terms supp and rigid are probably more appropriat since in bonsai we have a desire to ber the trunk and branches to produce a give shape.

Most beginners use young pla material. Trees that are two or three yea

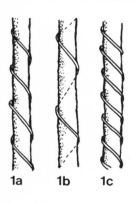

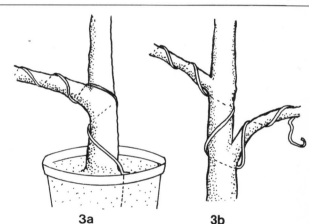

| 1a | 1b | 1c | 2 |

3a   **3b**

WIRING TECHNIQUES
Single Wiring
The angle for efficient bending is about 45 degrees, fig. 1a. Too widely spaced, fig. 1b, and the wire will not give sufficient support. Too closely spaced, fig. 1c, and the wire is wasted and will be a nuisance to apply and remove.

Double Wiring
Some trees respond with ease, others are difficult and may require the application of a second wire. When the second wire is applied, it should fit closely underneath the original wire, fig. 2.

When wiring a single branch, the end of the wire is anchored on the trunk or stem, or, as shown, in the pot, fig. 3a. Before placing the wire, the branch can be gently bent with the hand in the direction in which it is to be placed. The dotted line shows the position of the wire at the back of the trunk and branch.

Two branches in reasonably close proximity can be wired with one length of wire, fig. 3b.

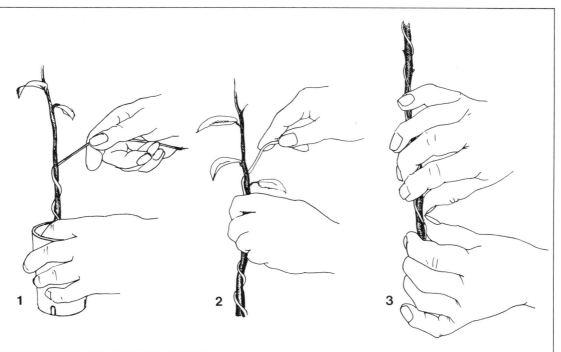

1   2   3

APPLICATION OF COPPER WIRE

The gauge of wire selected should be adequate to retain the shape once the stem or branches are bent. For standard work, this would be from 12-18 gauge. For very young and fine branches, a number 20 gauge is most suitable. There is no accurate way of measuring a length of wire for a given trunk or branch. It is considered more economical to unwind the coil of wire, make the application, then to cut the wire. (The length of wire in a coil is usually about 3 to 4 m.) The end of the wire is pushed to the bottom of the pot and anchored in the soil. The forefinger holds the wire at soil level whilst the first turns are applied. (Fig. 1)

The hand moves up the stem to give support to the piece of wood as the turns of the wire are applied. Note the angle and spacing of the turns and the fact that no leaves are caught in the wire. (Fig. 2)

The shaping of the wood is induced by pressure being applied on the wire. With fingers on the top and both thumbs close together underneath, gentle pressure is slowly applied and repeated until the wood responds. This is repeated along the trunk or branch until the desired shape is achieved. (Fig. 3)

ld are more flexible. But even at this tage it becomes obvious which wood is upple and which is rigid. Briefly, those rees belonging to the group known as onifers usually have supple or flexible ood; sometimes even when a conifer is even years old the trunk may be bent into hape. On the other hand, the broadleaf group of trees is considered to have rigid wood. This group includes Japanese maples, camellias and azaleas which all require wiring at an early age to produce good shape. Older trees may be bent but require very thick wire.

Elastic bands and weights hanging on the ends of branches are sometimes used to bend wood, but these methods lack the efficiency of applied wire and cannot be said to really shape a branch.

When is the Wire Applied?

As the summer temperatures increase, plant growth will decrease, and by the end of summer or early autumn the year's growth should have been completed. This is the time to apply wire and begin bending and shaping. When shaping trees with tender bark, the wire can first be wrapped in rice paper to prevent damage.

Duration of Wiring

Hardly any two trees will respond in the same way, thus no cut-and-dried rules can be formulated for the length of time that wire should remain on a plant. It can be two to three months in the case of small branches, and four to five months for larger branches. If the bark is not damaged by the wire it may be left on for as long as a year. On some occasions when the wire is removed a branch will slowly revert to its original position and will need rewiring the following wiring season. If wire is left on during the time of actual growth or applied just prior to the growing season, it could bite into the stem or branch and damage or disfigure the plant.

Removal of the Wire

When it is assumed that the wood has matured to the desired shape, the wire can be removed. There are two methods: the first is unwinding the wire, taking care not to damage foliage or buds; the second is to cut the wire at intervals along its length and allow it to fall off. The latter is by far the safest way and Japanese wire-cutters are specifically designed for such work to be carried out without damage to the stem.

Accidental Breakage

The fracturing or breaking of the piece of wood being bent will probably give rise to the most awful noise ever to be heard in bonsai culture. The immediate reaction can well be the feeling of despair generally occasioned by complete disasters. But take heart, most of these breaks are usually only fractures as the wire may prevent a complete severing of the wood. If this is the case, rejoin the fracture as accurately as possible, then smear the wound with a sealing compound — petroleum jelly will do. Lastly, tightly wrap it with grafting tape or some substitute, for an airtight and watertight seal. This will aid the healing of the union which may take 12 to 20 weeks or more. Once the fracture is healed, make no attempt to rebend the wood at that spot. If the break is complete, then unwire the tree, clean the wound and seal it. Then give serious thought to redesigning the tree.

Pruning

Pruning is carried out for several reasons, each one of particular importance in bonsai work.

The first is to force the production of new branches. This is an essential step with young seedlings where few, if any, branches exist. First the terminal shoot is cut out, and it is important to remember that once the growing tip of the trunk is severed, the trunk will never grow again. Yet the plant may not have reached the desired height. Its shape will also be less than perfect. Both calamities can be remedied easily by training the topmost branch to become the new leader. It would automatically assume this role, but for bonsai work it will need wiring to ensure a smooth alignment with the trunk. If more branches are desired, the new leader can itself be cut. It too will never grow again and a new leader must again be trained. The younger the tree, the more vigorous the growth, so after possibly five or even 10 years, the need to cut out the leader will be reduced.

Pruning is also carried out to encourage branches to grow in a given direction. Once the terminal bud is pruned from a side branch, a new branch will shoot from the next bud found in the axil between leaf base and branch. If that bud is on top of

Tip pruned to produce a magnificent floral canopy, this red azalea
is a focal point in the Omiya Nursery, Japan, in spring.

A 170-year-old five-needle pine, *Pinus parviflora.*
The heavy pot with additional soil counterbalances the weight
of the semi-cascade style branches.

This cascade style five-needle pine, *Pinus parviflora*,
on show in the School of Horticulture, Tokyo,
is over 210 years old.

Top: In entrance ways visual impact is important.
Miniature bonsai can be arranged in a single row to give an eye-appealing display.
Bottom: Bonsai are best displayed on table-height benches.
An unusual alternative used in a Japanese nursery is a water table
which has the added advantage of maintaining plants in a moist atmosphere.

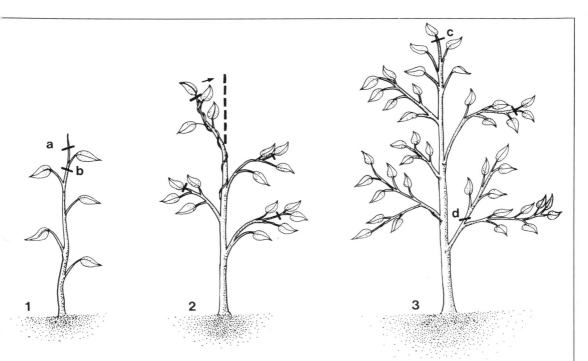

PRUNING A SEEDLING

A year-old seedling is pruned at either (a) or (b) to induce branching. (Fig. 1)

One year later, branches have developed. The trunk, once cut, will never grow again, so to meet the requirements of most bonsai styles, a side branch must be trained to become the new leader. The tips of the branches are pruned to induce new branchlets. (Fig. 2)

In its third year the new leader has grown in length and produced a new branch. Side branches grow in the direction of the bud to which they were pruned. The bottom branch, which was more severely pruned, has grown more vigorously. (Fig. 3)

Severe pruning now at (c) could induce desirable branching between the top and second branch.

The vertically growing branch at (d) is removed completely. Only those branches growing from underneath or the sides of branches are retained in bonsai work.

e branch, the shoot will grow towards e vertical; if the bud is at the side, the oot will grow towards the horizontal, ile a bud beneath the branch will gener- ly shoot out both downwards and out- rds as well as towards the light. Thus a anch is tip-pruned to the bud that will oot in the direction most desirable for e bonsai shape being crafted.

Once a plant is mature, pruning is ed both to control size and to maintain ape. The continued pruning of outer tips induces branches which are essential for a dense leaf canopy — desirable in most bonsai styles.

Another important aspect of prun- ing in bonsai work is pruning to produce flowers — particularly important with azaleas, chrysanthemums, rhododendrons and the like, which are often grown for their flowering beauty. This is pruning that can generally be done with the fingers as it involves pinching out the flower buds which develop at the end of new growth

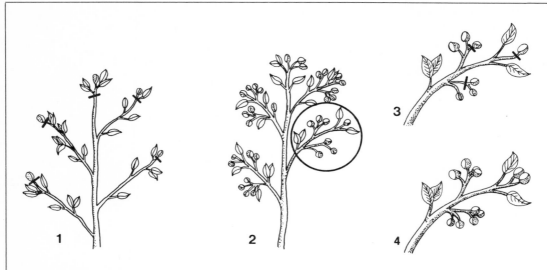

PRUNING FOR FLOWER PRODUCTION

A branch of a mature azalea, fig. 1. In late summer, each terminal branch bears a flower bud which, if left on the bush, will flower the following spring. These are removed back to the first or second leaf.

Within four to five weeks, new shoots will emerge, each bearing a flower bud, fig. 2. These too are removed, fig. 3. At this stage, fertiliser and water are applied, after which final growth for the year will be made.

Four to five weeks later, the flowers on one branch have been increased from one to 11, fig. 4. The length of the branches will be about two-thirds of their original size before pruning took place, thus the plant is encouraged not only to flower but also into a denser habit of growth suitable for most bonsai styles.

This procedure is applicable for most flowering trees except those that flower on fruiting spurs, like crabapples and ornamental pears.

during their growing period. A month after such pinching-out, two buds will have developed to replace the original one. With plants like azaleas, the process can then be repeated to encourage four flower buds where once there was one. This tip-pruning also reduces the length of the branch being pruned by about one-third, and thus a more compact habit of growth is achieved which in itself is desirable in most bonsai styles.

Pruning finesse will come as familiarity with each particular plant increases. The time of the year that the plant is pruned, for example, can be important. The select list of plants at the end of this

book gives guidelines on pruning times f[or] the most popular bonsai species.

Information on basic pruning tec[h]niques necessary for achieving the vario[us] shape classifications is given in the follo[w]ing section.

Training to Classification Ideals

Miniature Bonsai

Miniature bonsai may be started fro[m] seed specially sown for such work or fro[m] seedlings removed from the garden. Th[ey] are usually trained in small pots, say 5 c[m] propagating tubes, which help to control the size and the volume of the root, and make it much easier to transfer the plant to the ornamental pots.

It is a very slow process, taking years for the seedling to assume a tree-like shape, but it does have advantages, especially in the field of design as the flexible trunk allows for shaping into most classified styles. The foliage also often remains reduced in size.

Initial shaping can take place during the first year of growth. Root-pruning can be done when the seedling is a few centimetres tall or at the stage when it can be picked up between the thumb and finger. The growing plants in the propagating tubes will need some summer protection in the warmer zones.

Starting miniature bonsai from cuttings gives increased trunk diameter but cuttings are usually more rigid and thus lack the capacity to be shaped. Cuttings are thus generally ideal for the straight-trunk styles, such as formal upright and formal groups.

A third method is the severe pruning of roots, trunk and branches of an older tree. Some knowledge of the particular plant and its response to harsh pruning would be needed before embarking on such drastic work. There is little information recorded on this type of work. Those involved often spend many years testing and growing, and then consider the results as "their secret". But the following two examples of my own work may prove a helpful guide.

The first, a Japanese maple, 100 cm tall, was severely pruned to 10 cm above soil level. It had been root-pruned on two previous occasions and was growing in a 10 cm pot. The spring growth consisted of three new branches only and they were allowed to grow. At the end of summer, these branches were wired, the uppermost one was trained vertically as the new leader, the other two, which were luckily nicely spaced, were trained as branches giving the basic framework of the miniature tree which is now 14 cm high and has a spread of 14 cm.

The second was a seedling from an English hawthorn, 35 cm tall. Previously pruned, it was growing in a 10 cm diameter pot and had an attractive bend in the lower trunk almost from soil level. It was cut down to 15 cm from soil level. Once again, three new branches developed on the trunk and three new shoots came up at or slightly below soil level. In late spring, the original trunk was again pruned to the uppermost of the three new branches, which was 9 cm above soil level. This was wired vertically as the new leader, the other two as side branches. Two of the new shoots arising from soil level were cut off, leaving one which was wired and in a good position for use as a second trunk. In other words, a twin-trunk had been created.

This kind of work would be almost impossible on most of the conifers unless there already existed some small branches low down on the trunk. Severe pruning on leafless or branchless wood could be fatal.

Training of older trees of this sort continues for three or four years, after which an attractive little tree may be the result. At this stage it can be transferred to its ornamental bonsai pot. With the exception of conifers, most plants will respond to this type of treatment.

Most miniature bonsai are repotted annually. With experience, the grower will get to know the requirements of the individual plants, but the interval between repotting should not exceed two years. For those who lack the patience, seedlings may be planted into ornamental pots instead of training pots. In summertime these tiny pots with their equally tiny trees will need extra care.

Pruning to maintain the classified size is best done in spring. Then new shoots are cut to reduce their length. For example, if a shoot is 8 cm long and carries six leaves, it can be cut to 1 or 2 cm, leaving one leaf behind. With needle-like trees, it is better to nip or pinch out the growing bud, leaving a few needles only.

Small Bonsai

The process of development can follow closely that for the miniature trees, except

CLINGING TO A ROCK:
THE DISTANT MOUNTAIN VIEW

Once you have chosen which face of the rock will be the front, mark out the points on which the trees will be placed. Scrub the rock and allow it to dry. Holding wires — two, three or more per tree — are glued at these sites. Modern water-proof adhesives are efficient for this purpose. (Fig. 1)

A clay-mix type of soil is now smeared thickly on the rock surface where the trees are to be planted. The mix is made up of about 50 per cent clay wetted down to a slush and thoroughly mixed with 50 per cent well-rubbed-out peat or sphagnum moss. This sticks to the rock and is the basis for the root system to attach itself to the rock. (Fig. 2)

The trees are now prepared. Soil is removed to almost bare the roots. Some trimming of roots may be necessary, but some longer ones can be left and these will be placed at the back of the rock where additional soil is used. To protect the bare root from damage when the wire is tied, place a small pad of paper or sphagnum moss between wire and root wherever they cross. (Fig. 3)

A potting-mix soil is now used to cover the root. This is moistened so that it will remain in place, especially on the more vertical surfaces of the rock. The soil is now covered with moss. If available, large pieces are easier to keep in place and are preferred. The moss is held in place with copper wire shaped like a staple, 2-3 cm long. (Fig. 4)

Seen from the rear, the roots that have been placed at the back of the rock are treated the same as those in front — covered with soil and moss. Both are extended to the bottom of the rock to encourage the roots to grow downwards to the water in the *suiban*. (Fig. 5)

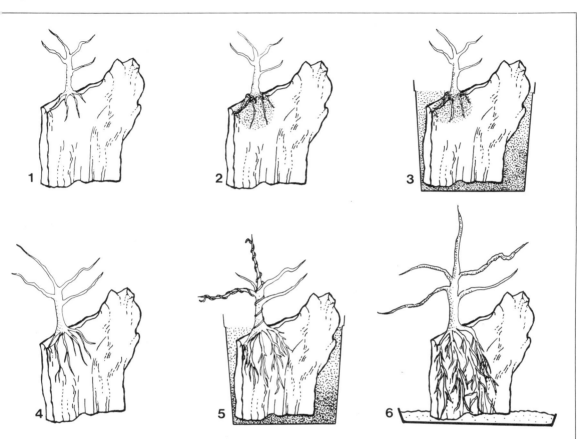

ROOT OVER ROCK STYLE

A seedling, once root-pruned to encourage secondary rooting, is bare-rooted and placed in position. The preparation of the rock is similar to that for clinging to a rock style. The seedling is tied in place and the root carefully arranged. (Fig. 1)

A clay-mix type of soil is added to keep roots in place. (Fig. 2)

The rock is now placed in a container or large pot and soil is added until the root is covered. It is now treated like a potted plant, remaining undisturbed for one year. (Fig. 3)

After a year, it is removed and the soil is taken away so that the progress of the roots can be seen. The new roots arranged, the original roots are checked to ensure that they are still close to the rock surface. The plant is replaced in the container. (Fig. 4)

This routine is repeated for three or four years. In the meantime, the trunk and branches are shaped and trained to suit the rock. (Fig. 5)

In about five years, the root can be systematically uncovered to expose the bark for hardening off. When the setting is satisfactory for exhibiting, it can be transferred to an ornamental bonsai tray. (Fig. 6)

that the initial planting can be in bigger pots, say, 10-12.5 cm diameter. This of course will increase the speed and size of the growth and, in comparison with the miniatures, the trees will tolerate greater exposure to the elements, and are much easier to look after.

Root-pruning will be necessary each year for the first three years; it then may be eased off to intervals of two to three years.

Medium Bonsai

Plants propagated from seed, cutting or layering, nursery-bought plants and plants removed from the garden are all potential medium-size bonsai material. The size of the pretrained plants will be governed by personal taste and skill. The following example of my own work may give an indication of the scope and timing involved in training this size plant.

A Moreton Bay fig grown from seed was root-pruned and potted in a 7.5 cm propagating tube. In the second year it was again root-pruned and planted in the garden. It had grown to a height of 17 cm. In each of the next three years it was lifted, root-pruned and replanted in the garden, but there was little or no pruning of trunk or branches. By the seventh year it was 3.4 m tall with a trunk diameter at soil level of 14 cm. The trunk was severely pruned to bare wood 35 cm tall and the tree was potted in a 30 cm diameter plastic pot. The root system was pruned to fit the pot. During the next two years it was repotted and new branches were trained. The following year, 10 years after its first root-pruning, it was transferred to an ornamental pot, rectangular in shape and measuring 40 cm long, 29 cm wide and 14 cm deep. The early training of the root system is now in evidence. Three beautiful buttress-like roots all presented in the ornamental pot give a superb aged look to the tree. They cover a spread of 30 cm. Future root-pruning could be expected at intervals of not less than three years.

Large Bonsai

Much like the previous size, semi-advanced trees can be trained. Similarl there are no limitations on the selection plant materials. In addition, flowering ar fruiting trees are at their best in this siz Camellias, magnolias and rhododendro are ideal among the flowering plants. A the citrus fruit trees, from grapefruit cumquat and persimmon, can be grown perfection. Plant material worldwide ca be accommodated in this classificatio especially those with larger leaves whic are unpopular for the smaller categorie The training programme is similar to th for the other sizes. Although it is a bigge tree, this does not necessarily mean that grows more quickly or that it requires di ferent treatment in pruning or shaping root-pruning.

Formal Upright Style

Most trees will normally grow in a vertic direction, so the formal upright tree wi require very little shaping. When the trun is approaching its approximate height, wayward leader may need straighteni up. It is unlikely that the trunk will nee any additional attention throughout i life. The branches, however, may nee more attention. Branches must join th trunk in an arrangement that is an upwa spiral. The lowest branch, always a sid branch, leaves the trunk on one side, th next branch leaves slightly higher fro the back of the trunk, the next branc leaves slightly higher from the opposit side and so on. On an untrained tree, it wi most probably be necessary to eliminat branches to achieve this arrangement. Th should be done after careful study of th plant to see which existing branches mos closely resemble the ideal; the rest shoul then be discarded. All the unwanted growt should be cut out, then each branch wired and shaped — straight and at righ angles to the trunk, thus giving th formality that the name suggests. Th branches can then be pruned to give a overall conical shape.

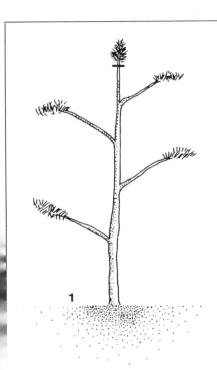

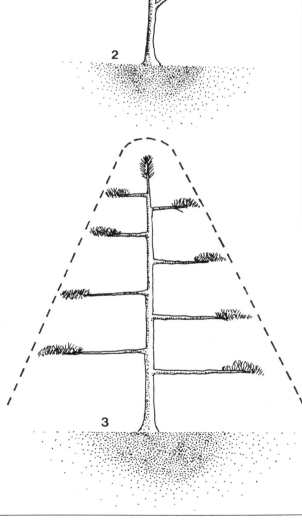

FORMAL UPRIGHT

Most trees, even at two years of age, will grow straight up with very few branches. The leading bud is therefore pruned and left for a year. (Fig. 1)

A year later, some branching will result from the pruning. The top branch is wired and trained vertically as the new leader. If further branching is required, this new leader can itself be pruned. Where there is a super-abundance, branches are selected to conform to the desired spiral placement on the trunk and the rest are cut off. (Fig. 2)

Remaining branches are wired horizontally. Note the overall pyramidal outline of the tree. Tip-pruning establishes and maintains this. (Fig. 3)

Informal Upright Style

As previously mentioned, this style may have curves or just an irregular shape. The latter can very often be its natural shape. Initial pruning may involve the elimination of branches so that the remainder radiate in the same kind of upward spiral as described above. The application of wire and shaping is done to suit the owner. The trunk is first bent gently, ideally so that a branch is positioned on an outer curve. The branches are then encouraged to curve gracefully. In this style, the branches do not emerge from the trunk in a stiff horizontal line but are wired to slope and curve. Examine the finished work carefully as some adjustments can be made at this stage to rectify obvious mistakes. It is your tree — it must appeal to you. Whilst many trees in nature have an informal shape and sloping trunks and may appear

to be ideal for bonsai, remember that in our work, where we are restricting the ultimate height of the trunk, the natural shape may not have time to develop.

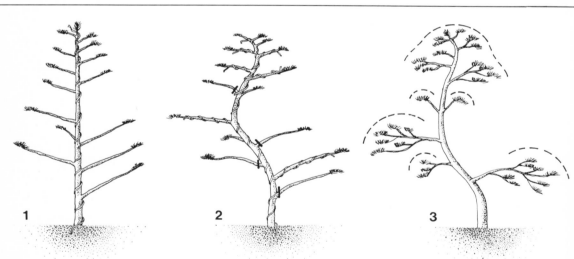

INFORMAL UPRIGHT

A three-year-old seedling is wired up the trunk for shaping into the informal upright style. (Fig. 1)

The trunk is gently curved but always the apex of the tree must be positioned directly in line with its base. Unwanted branches are pruned off, leaving branches emerging from the sides and back of the trunk and

emerging only from the outer curves except towards the top, where the arrangement is freer. (Fig. 2)

About a year later, branches develop and wiring can be removed. Tip-pruning will maintain the shape of the leaf canopy and increase its density. (Fig. 3)

Slanting-trunk Style

As previously mentioned, the top of the slanting-trunk style tree always turns upwards. There are no set rules to guide one as to the point of the trunk where the slant can begin. It can slant from ground level or part-way up the trunk. The angle — from 11 degrees to almost horizontal — can be induced by planting away from the upright or by wiring. The branches are trained parallel to the ground or angled slightly downwards. Towards the top of the tree, the normal branch arrangement prevails, that is, alternate branches or in groups of three.

Left: This five-needle pine in the informal upright style is over 150 years old.
Right: A Japanese maple, slanting-trunk style.

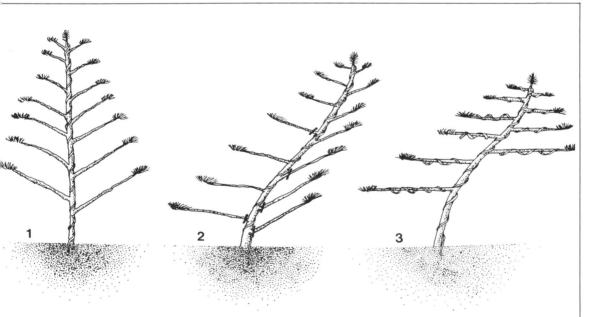

SLANTING TRUNK

The trunk of a seedling about three years old is wired. (Fig. 1)

The plant is then slanted and branches are removed from the underside of the trunk and to about one-third of the way up the trunk. At the top, they remain in the normal spiral arrangement, emerging from the sides and back of the trunk. (Fig. 2)

Branches are then wired into the horizontal and tip-pruned or allowed to grow into a lopsided pyramid shape. (Fig. 3)

Semi-cascade Style

To achieve this style a tree is wired and gradually bent in a horizontal plane. The branches that emerge from its lower side are pruned off. Branches arising from the upper side of the trunk give the appearance of a series of trunks and are, in fact, trained as individual trees. As with most styles, the aim is to produce a pyramid shaped leaf canopy, but within this there is considerable scope as the apex of the pyramid can be positioned above the bend of the trunk or anywhere along its horizontal length.

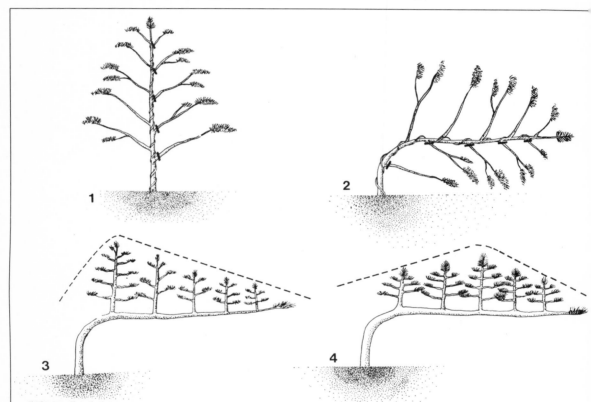

SEMI-CASCADE

The trunk of a seedling about three years old is wired. (Fig. 1)

The plant is bent at 90 degrees from the vertical and all the lower branches are removed. The upper left-hand branch is wired and will be trained into an independent tree-like shape. The remaining upper branches are in a good position and can also be wired to a vertical position. (Fig. 2)

Because it is nearest the root system and in a vertical line, the upper left-hand branch will normally grow more quickly than other branches. This forms the apex of the desired pyramidal shape. Branches are pruned to develop and maintain this shape. (Fig. 3)

A more unusual form of semi-cascade where the apex is formed on the extremity of the bent trunk. Semi-cascade styles like this usually arise following the natural development of branches. The pyramid shape is developed wherever it is easiest to achieve it. (Fig. 4)

ascade Style

his is virtually a weeping tree except that ... branches are trained similarly to ... pright trees, that is, horizontally and ... about 90 degrees to the trunk. The ... ranches arise from the front and the ... des and are pruned off at the back. In ... hat is called the formal cascade, the ... nd of the trunk is crowned with one branch trained into an independent tree not unlike an informal upright. Other cascades lack the crown, and on occasions one will see a cascade with only a few branches at the extreme end of the trunk, giving the impression of a very old tree. These are perhaps the more difficult styles to train and the least seen at exhibitions.

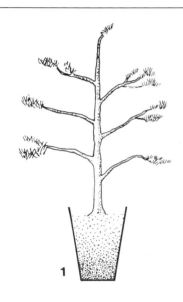

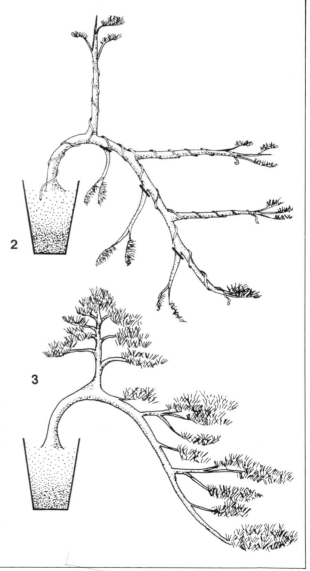

ASCADE

A seedling two to three years old is wired. Fig. 1)

t is then bent at an angle about 180 egrees. Underside branches are pruned off and the top branches are trained to the ertical at the apex, and horizontally for he length of the fall. (Fig. 2)

The ideal shape for a mature cascade, with he longest branches being found at the ottom and the shortest at the top. Thus esembling the natural growth of trees. Fig. 3)

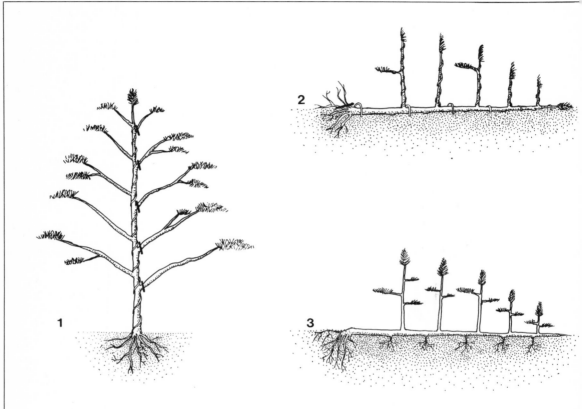

STRAIGHT RAFT STYLE

Here an advanced tree with many branches is used. All branches from one side are removed. (Fig. 1)

The remaining branches are wired straight, the tree planted horizontally and pegged to the ground by copper-wire hooks. (Fig. 2)

Two years later, the plant will have developed a new root system and the portion of old roots above the ground can be cut off. (Fig. 3)

Sinuous raft style is achieved in much the same way except that the tree is wired into an informal upright style before it is pruned and planted horizontally. Two-year-old seedlings are ideal being more flexible than more mature plants. After the first year, the plant is lifted and root-pruned. Two or three years later, sufficient branches will have developed to enable final selection for a good setting. The most suitable branches, those best positioned, are kept and wired into position. The rest are discarded.

aft Style

his is also an easy style to produce and
n be achieved using seedlings or more
ature plants. A seedling, say two years
d, where the stem has yet to produce
ranches, is root-pruned and planted
orizontally. The terminal bud is removed
stop elongation of the stem and at the
me time to encourage the production of
ranches. When roots have formed on the
ow horizontal stem, which may take one
two years, the original root system can
cut off. The raft is now dependent on
s new root system. The branches are
lowed to develop, most of which will
ow in a vertical pattern. Later, a number
these (usually an odd number) will be
lected as the main trunks; the unwanted
ranches will be cut off. An older tree may
used, taking advantage of existing
ranches which are wired at right angles to
e trunk, giving a more advanced look to
e setting.

atural Settings

hen a natural setting is first planted, the
ees are individually root-pruned, planted
d left undisturbed, usually for about two
ars. When the setting is lifted for its
rst repotting routine, it is treated as a
ngle tree, not separated into its individ-
l parts. The roots will very likely have
tertwined and root-pruning should not
sturb this too greatly.

Training the branches in a setting
volves pruning and wiring to develop an
erall shape consistent with the basic
ape of a single tree — that is, an
mbrella-shaped canopy. There are few
wer branches between the trees in the
tting, but outside branches may come to
ree-quarters of the way down the tree.
ese branches can be wired to a horizon-
l or slightly pendulous position.

oot over Rock Style

eedlings are the easiest material to train
this setting. Their roots are quite supple
d will thus respond well to shaping in
e strict discipline of this style — there
ust be no obvious spaces between the

root and the rock. The major disadvantages of working with seedlings is that five
or six years can elapse before a plant is
ready for display.

Using advanced trees, four to five
years old, can both enhance the setting
and allow for earlier exposure of the roots.
The tree should be root-pruned two to
three times as part of its early training.
There is, however, a problem that arises
when working with more mature plants. At
this age the roots are beginning to lose
their suppleness and are more difficult to
force into exact contact with the rock's
contours, even with the aid of wire. There
is a way out of this: using the tools of the
stonemason, the rock can be shaped to fit
the roots. Small cold-steel chisels and a
small hammer are ideal, as excessive
hammering can shatter the rock.

Planting and training routines are
the same as those given for the seedling
(see diagram), but the plant could be ready
for display in about one to two years.

Clinging to a Rock Style

Intricate in its assembly, this style also
has special problems involved in its maintenance, because the volume of soil used
for each tree is generally less than that
used in a pot. The soil is therefore heavily
loaded with peat or other water-retentive
material. The tip of the root system is
allowed to grow down the rock and into
the water in the *suiban* (the ornamental
shallow tray lacking drainage holes). This
becomes an important lifeline, especially
during summer time. In high summer the
rock should not be exposed to direct sunlight as the heat is absorbed and helps to
dry the moisture in the soil.

Overall training of plants is any
pruning or wiring that will be consistent
with the final aim of producing a scene
that looks like a distant mountain view.

Cluster Groups

For cluster groups, individual trees are also first root-pruned. The group can be tied together at their base, planted and left for about 12 months, after which the string is cut. The group will naturally spray outward into a fan shape. Because they have been growing in such close proximity to each other, there will be little growth along each plant's trunk, but anything that is growing between trunks should be cut out up to at least one-third the height of the trunk.

Each tree is planted so close to the next one that the intertwining of roots will be rapid, so the setting can be root pruned after 12 months. Again, the setting is treated as an individual tree and the trees are not separated.

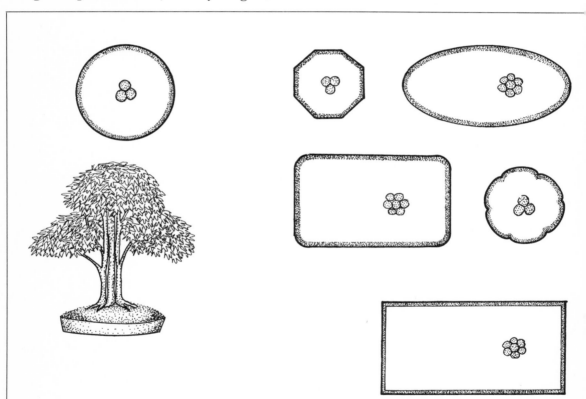

CLUSTERED GROUP STYLE

An uneven number of trees is tied together at the base, planted and left undisturbed for a year, after which the tie is removed. Trees are of a single species but can vary in age or be the same age.

Pots for this style can vary in shape. In addition to round pots, many-sided pots and those shaped like a flower are popular. Rectangular and oval pots can also be used, but rather than centring the group, it is placed at one-third in from one end of the pot.

Trees with the largest diameter are usually placed in the centre of the group with younger or thinner-stemmed trees surrounding them.

Clump Style

The clump style is one of the easiest multiple trunk styles, there being three simple methods of producing this style. The first is a result of severe pruning, either of a seedling or an advanced tree. It requires virtually cutting the tree down, the vital cut being made just above soil level. New shoots will arise in a whorl around the cut. Not all trees respond to this treatment but popular bonsai material like maples, Chinese elm, camphor laurel, zelkova, crabapple, cherry, fig, pyracantha and cotoneaster are usually successful.

A second method of producing this style is possible by aerial layering where multi-branches exist, especially the branch arrangement known as whorled. Tufted growth, where many shoots arise from a common point, can arise almost anywhere in a tree after severe pruning.

The third method makes use of a plant's natural growth habit. Most shrubs, for example, azaleas, have many branches arising from soil level — these can be dug up, the soil removed to root level and thereafter sufficient trunks are selected and trained.

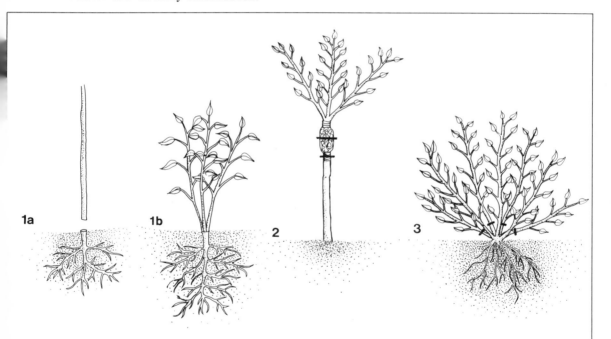

CLUMP STYLE

A seedling is severely pruned just above soil level, fig. 1a. It will send out shoots at soil level forming an effective clump, fig. 1b, which can be dug up, root-pruned and potted.

Multiple branches existing on the trunk of an advanced tree can be used. An aerial layer will produce roots, after which the whole section of trunk can be removed and planted. (Fig. 2)

A selected shrub can provide a ready-made clump style. Unwanted branches are pruned out, leaving three, five or seven. The shrub is then dug up, root-pruned and potted for further training. The shrub may need some reduction in height to suit a classified size. It will then be necessary to select the front and train the branches, now trunks, for a pleasing profile. (Fig. 3)

ROOT-PRUNING, POTTING AND REPOTTING
THIRD THE ROOTS

 It is in the care of a bonsai's roots that the secret of its longevity is found. Training of the roots begins early in the plant's life and involves three major routines — root-pruning, potting with the correct soil mix and a repotting programme.

Root-pruning

One of the important routines in bonsai culture is the pruning of the roots, firstly to train the root system to fit a shallow container, and secondly to control the root system once the tree is established in the ornamental bonsai pot. After pruning, new soil is supplied which is one of the main stimulants for increased life. The persistent root-pruning and the addition of new soil give the bonsai the potential of a lifespan well into hundreds of years.

Beginners in bonsai may need some encouragement when they approach their first root-pruning exercise, since most horticultural publications warn gardeners against disturbing root systems. We are told, for example, that "seedlings should be handled with great care so as not to damage the delicate root system". As this and many more warnings are commonplace, it is no wonder that we are apprehensive about root-pruning. But in fact such pruning will not hurt the root system and, as will be seen, roots respond well to such treatment.

The functions of roots are to anchor the plants in the soil and absorb water and mineral nutrients from it. The roots also often serve as a food reservoir. There are two basic types of root system. The most common is profusely branched and referred to as a fibrous root system. Somewhat less common is the system made up of a single main root or taproot, normally penetrating deep into the soil. The main root of young seedlings is known as the primary root and the branches which

arise from this are called secondary roots. When seedlings are allowed to grow unimpeded for one year, the primary root is usually greater in length than the stem above soil level. For bonsai work, this vast growth is obviously undesirable and the bonsai grower should not hesitate — this elongated taproot can be cut in half safely, in fact two-thirds may be removed safely.

The taproot will never grow again. In its place will be an increased number of secondary roots, and the process of repeated pruning will develop a root system not unlike the fibrous system. This conversion from a vigorous primary or taproot system into a compact fibrous system is what the bonsai grower should work to develop in all bonsai root systems.

There is little known about the extent to which the root system may spread in nature. Wheat roots have been

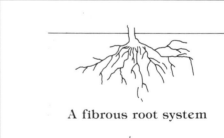

A fibrous root system

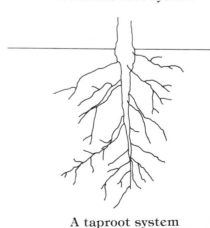

A taproot system

A fig, *Ficus rubiginosa*, root over rock style.

This twin-trunk style Japanese maple
is over 25 years old.

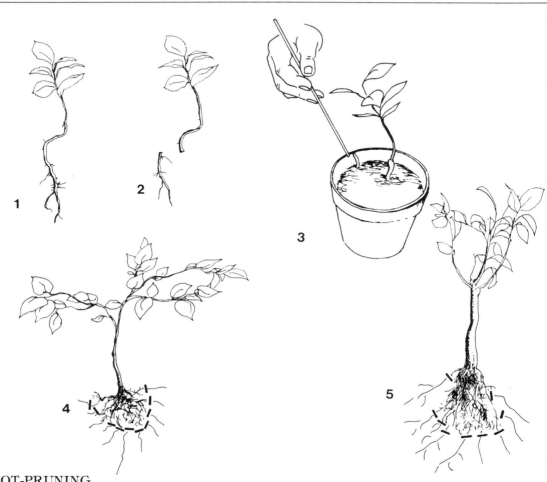

ROOT-PRUNING

The subject is a *Camellia sasanqua* seedling removed from the soil under the parent tree. It has a distinctive primary root with a few small secondary roots. The length of the primary root is greater than the stem. (Fig. 1)

The primary or taproot has been cut in half and both pieces are now ready for potting. (Fig. 2)

The now-potted seedling is accompanied by the lower portion of the taproot which could give rise to another plant. Note the small portion showing above soil level. (Fig. 3)

After three months no further growth of the primary root shows. In its place is the early development of the secondary roots which are root-pruned as shown. (Fig. 4)

After root-pruning at about three years. The stem is thickening together with a compact mass of secondary roots. Once again, it is obvious that the primary root or taproot has not extended and this fibrous-like root system is maintained by repeated root-pruning. (Fig. 5)

recorded penetrating the soil for 10 m or more. In bonsai culture, the root is trained into a compact rather than spreading mass, within the confines of a container, but this does not mean it stops growing. Roots grow in length only near their tips where there is a small area designated to be the region of elongation. These tiny roots, the tips of which are protected with caps, are able to penetrate through heavy soils. At the back of the region of elongation is the area that produces the root hairs whose function is to absorb the water and nutrients on which the plant feeds. These grow in thousands but have a limited lifespan — older ones die and new ones carry on. It is a function of root-pruning, which artificially removes old root hairs, to force on the production of new ones and thus the plant's life-support system is maintained. Just how quickly new root hairs grow can be seen from the following two examples. A tree root-pruned in the middle of winter and placed on bottom heat regenerated hair roots in less than 10 days. Perhaps more remarkable was a rhododendron which was root-pruned in the middle of winter, wrapped in hessian and left fully exposed. Root hairs were visible on the outside of the hessian wrapping in 10 days. In spring this regeneration would have been much quicker.

When to Root-prune

The interval between root-pruning can be one to two years for younger vigorous-growing trees, up to five years for more mature trees and perhaps 10 years for very old trees.

One of the main indicators that root-pruning is necessary is when the soil level in the pot appears to be very close to the rim. Continued root growth accumulating in the bottom of the pot pushes the root ball upwards and with it the soil. It is very obvious in neglected pots where the soil level may be nearly 2 cm above pot level. Such a pot is difficult to water as the water runs off the surface and outside the pot,

instead of penetrating the soil.

Root-pruning and repotting act to prolong the life of a tree as new rich soil replaces the old soil at each repotting. The keen bonsai grower would never allow his or her trees to become root-bound.

Potting

Potting is the term used in horticulture for planting in containers. The plants may be seedlings, cuttings or semi- to advanced material growing in the open. In turn, the size of the pots will vary. In bonsai culture, seedlings and cuttings for miniature work are generally potted in the smallest propagating tubes with a diameter of about 5-7.5 cm. Some may have their first potting in 100-125 mm pots. Some may start off in the 100-125 mm pots, and, as the trees increase in age, and according to the forecast classification for size, finish up in 20-30 cm pots prior to their transfer to the ornamental containers.

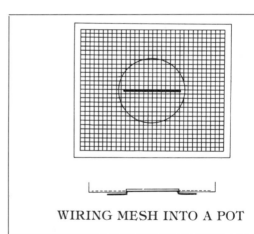

WIRING MESH INTO A POT

Soil

In selecting ingredients to make up potting soil, thought should be given to the nutrient value, the retention of moisture within the soil and the drainage of excess moisture to allow aeration and good drainage. Most soil formulae used in bonsai conform to this. The proportions of standard materials used in the mix, such as

rden loam, peat moss, compost and
nd, vary as a result of the origin of the
aterial, its physical structure or just to
it the person making up the soil.

One of the popular mixes in use
day goes under the name of the John
nes Potting Mix. The formula is as
llows: seven parts garden loam (topsoil),
ree parts peat moss or compost and two
rts sand.

The most variable item is the garden
am. It ranges from light sandy soil of
astal areas to heavy clay. Both are
desirable extremes in pot culture, for
hich the obvious choice would be a sort of
agical medium loam that rarely exists.
overcome this, a potting mix formula
ust be flexible, with increased sand for
avy loams and increased peat for the
ry sandy soils. Each bonsai grower must
ggle the formula to suit his or her own
eds.

eat Moss Today this is in plentiful
pply, and a choice is available. Some
rieties, like German peat, are being
ed as basic soils with sand alone being
lded to improve the drainage.

ompost The keen gardener may substi-
te material from the compost heap in
ace of peat.

nd For countless years we have been
ainwashed that coarse, sharp sand is a
ust for garden use, but sand is sand. If
u have access to fine sand, use it.

The quantities of the various in-
edients are by volume. A flowerpot can
used for measuring and, like making a
ke, the ingredients must be thoroughly
ixed.

To test the mix, fill a flowerpot, say
5 mm size, and lightly compact the mix
though firming the soil when planting.
en apply water till it runs out the
ainage holes. It is important to note that
odern horticultural techniques do not
prove of the use of dirty pieces of
oken clay flowerpots being placed in a
t as drainage material. The soil formula
so well calculated that it allows the
ter to drain freely from the soil without
y help. Also, the modern pot is so

designed to allow free drainage of surplus
water without the loss of soil.

The pot should then be placed in the
open with access to sun and normal atmospheric conditions. Allow the surface to
dry, then test it. Has the soil surface caked
hard dry? Is the surface loose with particles
of sand, soil and peat? Now rewater and
watch the speed of absorption. If the
water does not move freely, remix the soil
with additional sand, then retest. Repeat
until the mixture is satisfactory. A valuable bonsai can be set back severely with a
bad soil mix.

Ready-mixed potting soils are freely
available today, but quality varies. If the
switch is made to a new mix, it is a good
idea to keep a record of its performance
for future reference.

Repotting

Repotting is the term used in bonsai for
the removal of the tree from a training or
ornamental pot, pruning the roots, reducing the old soil, and replacing the tree with
new soil in the same pot or into an ornamental pot.

Repotting into an Ornamental Pot

Before placing a tree for the first time in
an ornamental pot, the pot should be critically assessed. Marks, imperfections and
level of glaze will determine which is the
best-looking side to become the "front".
The tree that has already been trained
with a "front" is now placed and adjusted
in the pot.

In a round or square-shaped pot, it
is placed accurately in the centre. In oval
or rectangular pots, its position should be
one-third from one end of the pot. Right-
handed people may favour the tree in the
right-hand end of the pot, and *vice versa*,
or the tree itself may dictate its best
position. Where there is an extended lower
branch on the left-hand side, the tree will
be placed to the right-hand end of the pot,
and *vice versa*.

An eye-level view of a newly positioned tree may show it is sunk in the pot

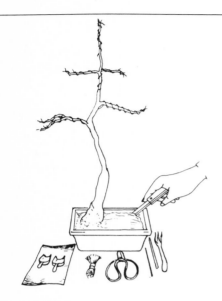

Place a layer of bonsai potting soil in the pot and level it with the mossing brush.

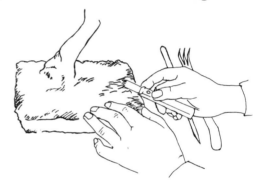

REPOTTING

This tree was potted three years ago and is now ready for repotting. The foliage was weather-beaten and suffered some insect damage, so the tree was defoliated as part of the repotting routine. The tools required are shown. The tree is removed from the pot by running a knife blade round the edge of the soil where it meets the inside of the pot. Using the knife blade as a lever, lift up the root ball. As soon as there is sufficient space, slide the fingers underneath the root ball and lift the tree out.

With the general-purpose knife, lift off the moss. It can be re-used if in good condition. If the moss is showing signs of wear, scrape it off with the soil and dispose of it.

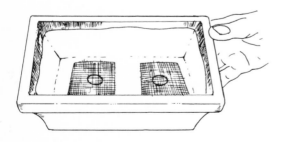

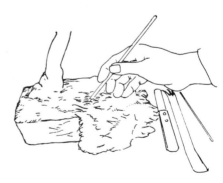

Clean the pot and prepare it to receive the root-pruned tree. Cover the drainage holes with plastic mesh, which may be secured with fine copper wire.

With the potting stick or cultivator, remove the upper and side layers of soil from the root ball. The amount of soil to be removed should be about one-third of the original total volume.

traighten out the roots. With the root-
runing shears, cut all exposed roots. This
:aves a neat-looking block of soil and
oot.

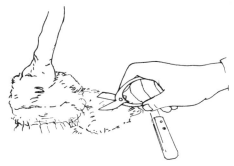

ilt the tree and remove more soil from
ie bottom of the block, about 1 cm would
o for miniatures, up to about 5 cm for
igger trees. Bring the root-pruning shears
ito action again and cut off all exposed
oots. In all, about two-thirds of the soil
olume has now been removed.

the tree is soiled or grimed, now is the
me to scrub it. Have ready an old
othbrush and a container of fresh water
which has been added a squirt of house-
ld detergent. Starting from the top,
ghtly scrub, taking care of buds or newly
xpanding branches. Do not damage the
ark with too vigorous a motion — gentle
rubbing is needed. Scrubbing can be
ore prolonged at the base of the trunk
id on any roots emerging there where the
ark is more mature and usually dirtier.
n completion, wash down with fresh
ater and allow any surplus water to drain
vay.

Replace the tree ensuring its base is
visible at eye level, and fill the pot with
new bonsai-potting soil. Firm it to help
anchor the tree. Then, with the aid of the
miniature trowel shape and lightly com-
press the soil to achieve an attractive
profile from the base of the tree to the
ends of the pot.

Water thoroughly without disturbing the
shaped soil. A misting spray is ideal for
this as no flooding of the soil takes place
and the water is absorbed quickly.

The moss should be reapplied without too
much soil attached to it. Before reapplying
old moss, it can be dunked in a mild
household disinfectant, which will also
remove a quantity of soil, and then rinsed
in fresh water. Moss should be lightly
pressed onto the soil surface for good
contact and the whole surface area should
be watered.

or it may even be well above the level of the pot. When presenting a tree in a shallow pot, its base should be clearly visible above the level of the pot, the base and upper part of its roots exposed. Usually the tree appears to be growing on a slightly raised mound of soil. The maximum height of this mound is about equal to the depth of the pot. For older trees planted in deeper pots, the soil is often level and sufficiently below the rim to allow for efficient watering, yet at the same time producing an attractive view of the base of the tree.

Trees being potted for the first time in an ornamental pot may lack stability because their root system is still in the early stages of training. To overcome this, the tree can be tied in with copper wire. The wire should be passed up through the drainage holes in the early preparation of the pot, before the soil is added. When the tree is placed in position, the wires are brought over the root ball and tied securely by twisting. The surplus wire is then cut off.

A finishing touch of moss as a ground cover is usually applied. This functions to enhance the appearance of the bonsai. Perhaps more importantly, it prevents the soil being washed away by normal watering techniques or heavy rain and, if well applied, it will even tolerate thunderstorm. Moss also prevents rapid evaporation of moisture from the soil surface during hot weather.

A repotted bonsai needs a safe shady spot, protected against strong winds and heavy rain for about two weeks. It should by then be settled in and can be replaced in its normal position.

Emergency Repotting
Emergency repotting usually has to take place after storms, violent winds or when accidents cause pots to be broken.

The immediate remedial action is to protect the root system from drying out. The tree can be placed in the garden, wrapped in hessian, or the root ball can be placed in a plastic bag, container or wooden box. If the tree has not been damaged, the bonsai can remain in it temporary position for some time until new pot is obtained.

Repotting into the new pot does no necessarily mean that the bonsai need any root-pruning. This may depend on th interval of normal repotting. Howeve you can take advantage of the emergenc action to carry out a normal repotting ro tine, bearing in mind the condition of th tree and the time of the year that repottin is normally necessary.

Good after-care is probably of mor importance than any other factor. Kee the repotted plant out of drying wind heat or cold. Recovery can be encourage by the use of a glasshouse or temporar structure with frequent misting of th foliage and a reasonably stable temper ture, both day and night.

PROPAGATION

There is generally great satisfaction in being able to propagate your own plant material and even profound pleasure in successfully nurturing a plant from seed to maturity. In bonsai there are also advantages in working with such young and malleable material.

Growing Bonsai from Seed

On a number of occasions I have watched students jumping up and down with joy when viewing their first successful seed-sowing — tiny seedlings showing their seed leaves (cotyledons) above the soil. This may infer that growing plants from seed is a difficult process. Not so, but it is a slow, long-term programme which nevertheless has some advantages, particularly in bonsai work. No special equipment is necessary and it is a cheap and fairly reliable method of producing new plants in quantity. From a purely bonsai point of view, it gives rise to a beautiful, naturally shaped tree, as opposed to plants grown by cuttings which use straight pieces of wood.

Collecting the Seed

Locate the trees from which you would like to harvest the seed. Find out at what stage the seed can be considered "ripe" and note the time for collection, which could be from late summer through to early winter. The select list of plants at the end of this book gives this information for the most popular bonsai species.

If the seed is contained in soft fleshy fruits — for example, pomes, berries and the like — colour will usually indicate harvesting time. Deep yellow, orange, red, scarlet and, on rare occasions, white and blue are the accepted ripe colours for such trees as cotoneaster, pyracantha, hawthorn, crabapple, cherry, plum, fig, blueberry ash and citrus. Having collected the fruit, dispose of the flesh, wash the seed clean, dry it thoroughly and store until late-winter sowing. Most of the seed will store for more than one year, sometimes as long as six years, but little information has been recorded on this.

With seed contained in pods or capsules or individually exposed seeds, some of which may have wings on them, ripeness is partly related to colour and partly to dryness of the outer coating. Colours range from dark green, browns of various shades, to red tints and even brighter colours on rare occasions. Such seeds should be collected and placed in dry storage where the capsules or pods will probably split open and discharge the seed in time for sowing. Though most seed is best sown in late winter, some may require sowing as soon as possible after collection. Acorns from oak trees are often recommended for early sowing in autumn.

A strong brown paper bag tied tightly at the top to keep out any vermin is ideal for this purpose. It is most important that whatever container is used for the storage of the seed must be dry and the seed must dry naturally. Any moisture will lead to the development of fungus, making the seed useless. Glass and plastic containers are the worst offenders.

Plants producing the non-fleshy seed containers include Japanese maple, ash, beech, elm, jacaranda, azalea, brachychiton and wisteria. For those who may have difficulty in collecting their own seed, seek advice from botanical gardens, local garden clubs or specialist groups, especially the bonsai clubs. Most big cities have seed merchants, most likely for commercial quantities, but there is no harm in trying them. Some bonsai nurseries may stock selected seed.

Germination

The process of germination is initiated by moisture entering through the seed coat. The environment in which the seed is sown, the ingredients making up the seed-sowing soil mix, and the care taken in planting the seed all assist in the initial process. On rare occasions, further help may be needed to assist the seed in the germination process. One method important in bonsai work is stratification.

Stratification

Some cold-climate seed may need cold storage when the trees are grown outside their normal climatic zone. Maples are a good example. *Acer palmatum*, the Japanese maple, when grown in a temperate zone will flower and produce seed, but rarely does the seed germinate. It is said to require overwintering, but the winter temperature in the temperate zones may be inadequate. This is a species that responds well to stratification.

The seed should be collected about the beginning of autumn. The wings are removed and the seed is then placed in moist peat or sphagnum moss. This should then be placed in a plastic bag and sealed. A label can then be tied to the bag, giving the date of stratifying, type of seed and number. Place it in the refrigerator (not the freezer) for a period of not less than 60 days up to about 150 days.

On rare occasions and sometimes when left too long, germination will take place in the refrigerator. In mid- to late winter, the seed should be viewed frequently. At any sign of swelling, the seed must be taken out and sown. Seedlings germinated in these cold conditions are very tender and will most likely collapse when planted and placed outside in normal atmospheric conditions, so they must be treated with care.

Sowing Mediums

Nowadays we look to the clean, simple mixes like peat moss and sand — 40 per cent peat and 60 per cent sand would be a reasonable medium. The peat, which has previously been moistened, is rubbed between the hands and reduced to small particles, then this is thoroughly mixed with the sand. If there are any doubts about the cleanliness or origin of the sand, it can be washed in a bucket with running water. It should be stirred and washed until the water is clean. The sand mixes better if it is reasonably dry.

Seed-sowing

Place the sand/peat mix in a clean pot and fill it to the top without compressi[ng] Level off, removing any surplus. Ligh[tly] press the mixture until it is level, abou[t] cm from the top; the surface should [be] smooth.

If large enough to handle, pick [up] each seed and place it on the surface, w[ith] no two seeds touching each other. [De]pending on quantity, the seed can [be] spaced evenly until it is used up. Tiny se[ed] which is difficult to handle may be sown [by] placing a quantity in a piece of clean pap[er] folded in half. Hold one end of the pap[er] over the pot and tap with a finger — t[his] wil cause the seed to flow along the crea[se] and spill out. Move the paper to give [an] even distribution.

Covering the Seed Burying the seed t[oo] deeply is often the cause of failure. T[he] reason for covering the seed is firstly [to] keep the environment around it moist [as] an aid to germination; and secondly [to] anchor the seed against movement aft[er] watering or heavy rain. As a guide [to] covering the seed, a simple formula is [a] layer about two to four times the diamet[er] of the seed. Admittedly this may be diffi[ffi]cult to judge accurately for very tiny se[ed] where a fairly light sprinkling is all th[at] will be required. An easy method [of] covering seed is to use a flour sifter. F[ill] with a fairly dry sand/peat mixture a[nd] shake it over the pot until the seed [is] covered.

Watering the Seed A fine-rose waterin[g] can or a garden syringe should be used [to] water the seed to avoid large volumes [of] water which will disturb them.

Once germination takes place, t[he] seedlings can be watered with a fungicid[e] This should help reduce the chances of t[he] common seedling disease, "damping off[".]

Care and Maintenance Late winter, s[ay] the third month, is ideal for seed-sowi[ng] and the propagation of future bons[ai] plants by the use of seed. The pot [or] container should be put in a shelter[ed] position on a clean, level surface. [Un]expected heavy rain may cause flooding [of] the container and if the pot is on a slopi[ng] surface, the seed will be washed to t[he]

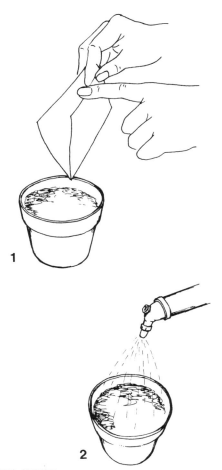

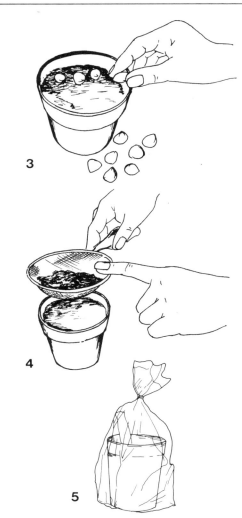

INE SEED

. clean pot of 100 mm or 125 mm iameter is prepared by filling with a eed-sowing mix, then lightly compressed ntil it is level, about 2 cm from the top. iny seed which is difficult to handle may e placed in a piece of clean paper folded half. Hold one end of the folded paper ver the pot and tap with a finger. This will ause the seed to flow along the crease and ill out. Continue tapping until seed is sed up or sufficient is sown. (Fig. 1)

o covering is placed over the tiny seed; atering is carried out by using a mist-rayer which does not disturb the seed. ig. 2)

LARGER SEED

Large seed is placed in position by hand, care being taken not to pack it too closely. (Fig. 3)

A covering two to four times the diameter of the seed in depth is added. This is of fairly dry seed-sowing mix, finely rubbed down and spread with the aid of a flour sifter. The pot is then watered.

The seed pots are now placed inside a clean plastic bag and sealed. Labels recording the date and name of the seed should be placed in each pot.

lower side, or even washed over the side.

Germination is evident when tiny green shoots are visible on or above the soil surface. Do not allow these to dry out. As progress is made and as soon as the seedlings are big enough to handle — that is, able to be picked up with the thumb and finger — they may be removed, root-pruned and potted for growing on.

With such tiny seedlings, root-pruning would consist of the removal of the growing point, a mere millimetre or two. That is sufficient to stop the development of a taproot, even in the most vigorous plants, and to encourage the growing of a fibrous-like root system.

Growing Bonsai from Cuttings

There are also advantages in propagating bonsai material from cuttings and there are few plants that do not respond to this method of propagation. Cuttings are usually true to flower, fruit and foliage of the parent tree and will flower at a reasonably early age in comparison with plants raised from seed. Under home-propagating conditions, cuttings will generally produce a root system within three months.

Cuttings are divided into three categories. First are the soft-tip cuttings, taken about six weeks after the commencement of spring growth. They are soft and succulent and not specially recommended for bonsai work.

Second are the semi-hardwood cuttings, taken in early summer — they are about 12 weeks old. This type of cutting is the most popular. Azaleas, camellias, most conifers, some maples, cotoneaster, pyracantha, zelkova, figs and many native trees will respond to this method.

The third category is the hardwood cutting, taken in autumn and winter. Such plants as wisteria, quince, pomegranate and figs should be cut at this time.

Preparation of Cuttings
Semi-hardwood Cuttings   These are taken

from the new shoots in early summer. T[ ] terminal ends should be intact about 7- [ ] cm long. Select from clean, health[ ] looking twigs of about the same length [ ] render a uniform group of plants.

A piece of bark is then cut from t[ ] base of the cutting, about 2 cm long, a[ ] about one-half to two-thirds of the leav[ ] are removed. The cuttings are then dipp[ ] in water, removed and the surplus wat[ ] shaken off.

Each of the cuttings should then [ ] dusted with a hormone rooting powde[ ] The easiest way is to insert the cut end [ ] each cutting into the powder, tap lightly [ ] remove excess powder and then plant [ ] the pot.

The cutting medium can be som[ ] thing like half-sand and half-peat, th[ ] oughly mixed. The peat should be moi[ ] and rubbed out to a reasonably fin[ ] particle size.

A standard plastic pot, 100 mm [ ] 125 mm, can be filled to the top wi[ ] cutting soil and lightly tamped down to [ ] smooth, level surface. The prepared cu[ ] ings are now inserted. A potting stick c[ ] be used to make the holes for the cutting[ ] which should be lowered into the mediu[ ] until the leaves touch the soil. The spacir[ ] and position of the cuttings may suit t[ ] individual — they may be placed in straig[ ] lines or follow the shape of the pot, or th[ ] may be packed in close together or space[ ] On completion, the pot and cuttings shou[ ] be thoroughly watered, surplus wat[ ] drained out, and the pot placed in a plast[ ] bag and sealed. To initiate root growth, t[ ] cuttings need an atmosphere of 100 p[ ] cent humidity, a condition which is su[ ] plied by the sealed plastic bag.

Do not forget to record the date [ ] the work, the name of the plant and a[ ] other details which may be of some valu[ ] when the work is repeated. The pot [ ] cuttings should be placed in a shady spo[ ] Under no circumstances should the leav[ ] of the cutting be exposed to direct su[ ] light, especially during the heat of the da[ ]

There is no special signal to indica[ ] the production of roots. Sometimes eve[ ]

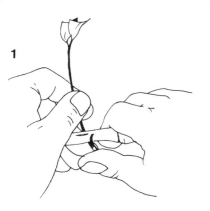

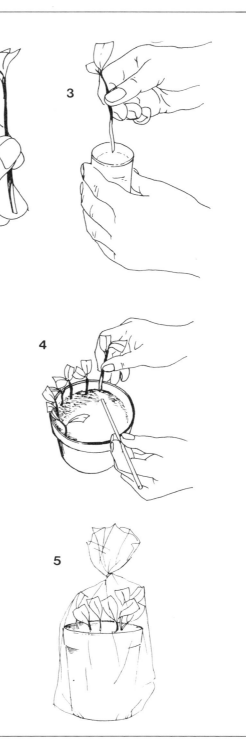

PREPARATION OF CUTTINGS

Semi-hardwood cuttings from this season's growth about 7-10 cm in length, are selected from clean, healthy-looking twigs in mid-summer. A piece of bark about 2 cm long is cut from the base end. All leaves except the top two are removed. These are cut in half to reduce "transpiration", thus keeping the cutting turgid and assisting in keeping the wood viable. (Fig. 1)

The bottom end of the cutting ready for dipping. (Fig. 2)

The exposed wood at the bottom of the cutting is now dipped in water then into a hormone powder. This will help in the development of the root system. (Fig. 3)

To prevent the hormone powder being rubbed off when forced into the cutting mix, a dibbler or potting stick is used to create a cavity for each cutting. (Fig. 4)

For the home gardener who lacks propagating aids (like a glasshouse, automatic misting and bottom heat), the pot of cuttings may be placed inside a suitable plastic bag. The cuttings have been watered and the bag is sealed to create a humid environment, an aid in keeping the cuttings alive. Keep the pot warm but not in direct sunlight. In about 12 weeks, some roots should have developed. (Fig. 5) new leaves on a cutting do not necessarily mean that roots have developed. Under home conditions, it may take anything up to 12 weeks for roots to appear. The only way to find out is to test the cutting by trying to lift it. If it resists pulling, one can assume that some roots have grown. Test a number at random spacing. If all resist, then assume they can be taken out and root-pruned. They can then be planted into individual pots for growing on, using a good, formulated potting soil similar to that used for potting bonsai.

Hardwood Cuttings Hardwood cuttings are often represented as being taken from deciduous trees only, which is not so. However, the time of collection usually coincides with leafless twigs. They therefore do not require the detailed care of the semi-hardwood types.

The cuttings may be up to 20-25 cm long. For uniformity of future plants, all cuttings should be undamaged terminal shoots of that year's growth. About 2 cm of bark should be removed on one side of the cutting at the bottom, similar to the routine for the previous cuttings. The tip should then be dipped in the hormone rooting powder. Planting can be made in open ground or in pots.

The leafless cuttings from deciduous trees can also be packed in bundles in boxes of moist peat moss for callus development over winter. They can then be lifted out at about the end of winter and treated as ordinary cuttings, that is, planted out in pots for root development.

Some hardwood cuttings can be wrapped in two or three layers of wet newspaper after normal preparation. They are then placed in a warm spot for forcing the development of roots. Bottom heat in a glasshouse is perfect. After leaving them undisturbed for the first three weeks, the bundles of cuttings should be unwrapped at weekly intervals for inspection. Root formation is often rapid, and those which show roots can be taken out, lightly root-pruned and then planted for growing on.

There are two disadvantages here.

Firstly, the warm humid conditions m encourage fungus. This can be overcor by washing the cuttings in a prepar fungicide before they are wrappe Secondly, buds may be forced into grow at the expense of the roots or emerge wi the roots. These new shoots are soft, su culent and tender and they may collap when exposed to normal atmosphe conditions.

Propagation by Layering

Of all the methods of propagation, laye ing is the most simple and often the mc successful for the non-professional. requires that the piece of wood remai attached to the parent tree until a rc system has been formed. It is then cut c and planted for establishing as a read made tree. A number of methods a available.

Simple Layer

A branch is brought down into contact wi the soil, a portion of bark on the undersi may be removed and the area painted wi a thick solution of water and hormo rooting powder. The branch is pegg down, or otherwise held against mov ment, covered with soil and left develop a root system. On occasions, t root will develop quickly within a fe weeks. Autumn is the best time to p plants propagated in this way, so it is well to carry out the work of preparation late winter or early spring, and no lat than early summer.

Mound Layer

This method is applied to those plan often referred to as shrubs, that ha many branches arising from the so Selected branches can be prepared cutting the bark close to soil level a painting the cuts with hormone past Then a prepared soil with the characte istics of a potting mixture should poured over the branches until it forms mound of soil deep enough to generous cover the wounded portions. It is th

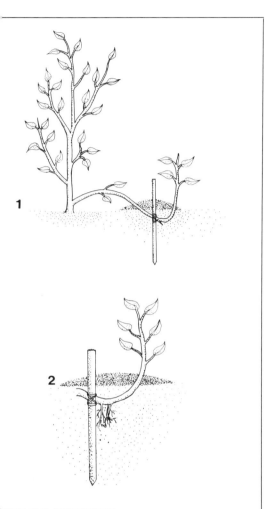

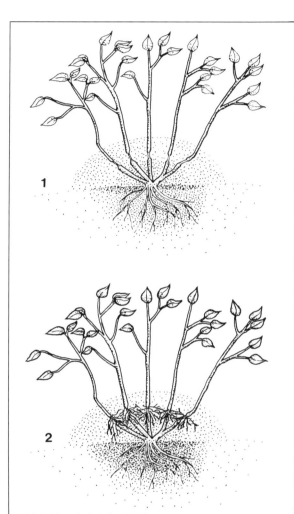

[SI]MPLE LAYERING

[A] branch is brought down to soil level [wh]ere it can be held firmly with a stake, [fig]. 1. The soil area is prepared with a rich [soi]l or compost and the branch is slashed [par]t-way through at the bend. This will [ass]ist bending and staking, but is also [ess]ential as the wound is the area in which [roo]ts could develop in about six to ten [we]eks. However it is advisable not to [sep]arate plants from their parents until [aut]umn, fig. 2.

[wa]tered and left. No further care or [ma]intenance is required unless heavy rain [wa]shes the mound away.

MOUND LAYERING

Stems that are to be used are ring-barked with a sharp knife and painted with a hormone paste. A potting-mix type of soil is mounded over the wounds giving them good, thick cover, fig. 1. The mound is then watered and covered with a mulch of leaves. The soil should be left undisturbed for at least 12 weeks after which each stem will have developed roots, fig. 2, and can be severed and planted independently.

Preparation can begin in early spring. Then in autumn the soil can be scratched or washed away for inspection of root development. If it looks adequate, cut the branches out and pot them individually. Replace the soil if branches are not ready for removal.

Aerial Layer

As the name suggests, this method requires the soil to be taken up to the branch to be rooted. All that is necessary is some method of holding the soil around the branch. One method can be a flower-pot cut in half, reassembled around the branch, tied in place against movement and filled with soil which will need frequent watering. Another method is to use a plastic bag or tube filled with peat moss, soil or other substitute. Both ends must be tied securely. The medium inside the bag should be moist. The most modern method is to keep the soil in place with a wrapping of aluminium foil, twisting bo[t]ends to seal the wrap. The advantage [of] these two latter methods is that there is [no] need to water the soil once in position. T[he] plastic or aluminium keeps the moistu[re] level constant.

In each case the bark on the bran[ch] should be cut and painted with t[he] hormone powder paste. The powder a[s]sists in the development of a better ro[ot] system.

Hormone rooting powder in varyi[ng] strengths is available at garden store[s]. Most brands give clear instructions on t[he] pack which should be followed carefully.

Layering techniques lend themselv[es] particularly well to bonsai production, a[nd] give greater scope than other propagati[on] methods. Large pieces of wood, up to [10] cm in diameter, can be rooted within [a] growing season. The result is a matur[e]

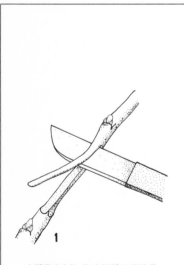
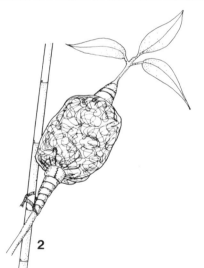

AERIAL LAYERING
A ring of bark 2-3 cm long is cut out of the branch. The wound is painted with a hormone rooting paste. The wound needs to be this large to prevent it healing before any roots emerge. (Fig. 1)

The wounded area is packed with damp peat or sphagnum moss. It is then wrapped in plastic or aluminium foil and secured with wire or tape at each end. (Fig. 2)

Roots will develop from the upper part of the cut in about six to ten weeks but the layer is best left undisturbed until autumn when the branch can be severed and planted independently. (Fig. 3)

oking tree with a trunk size that it could
ell take half a century to reach under
rdinary plant-growing methods.

ropagation by Root Cuttings

his is a form of propagation little men-
oned in modern horticulture, but one
articularly useful in bonsai work. Not
aly is it a simple and economical propa-
ation method — cuttings become avail-
ble when root-pruning is carried out —
it often the very shape of the root pieces,
ten unusual and naturally twisted, can
the basis for the style of the bonsai.

Cuttings 5 to 7 cm long, taken from
ots greater than 5 mm in diameter, can
oduce roots and shoots in a matter of
eks. Cossetted with propagating aids
e bottom heat, some cuttings will
ow in 14 days.

While it is generally accepted that
ere are no true buds on roots, a number
species have a root system suitable to
is method of propagation. In these
ants, growth on root cuttings arises not
m true buds but from adventitious buds,
d the new shoots are therefore called
ventitious shoots. Species traditionally

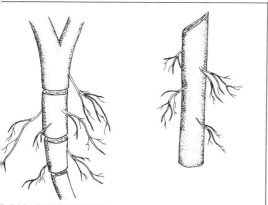

OOT CUTTINGS
piece of root from 5 to 10 cm long and at
ist 5 mm thick can be potted like a stem
tting except that root cuttings are
serted deeper into the soil with about
e-eight only of its length exposed.

propagated in this way include the elm,
flowering cherry, hawthorn, flowering
quince, ornamental pear, crabapple, ornamental peach and zelkova.

Despite the fact that the entire
length of a root cutting might previously
have been underground, it is now important that the correct end of the cutting is
the one to be reburied. This bottom end is
the one that was previously furthest from
the trunk. Root hairs are more likely to
form here, while shoots are more likely to
form on the end closest to the trunk. When
taking root cuttings, it is therefore important to make distinctive cuts on the top and
bottom. For example, the top can be angle-
cut and the bottom cut straight. Root
cuttings are potted deeper in the soil than
stem cuttings — about one-eighth of the
cutting is left exposed — but they are
prepared and protected in the same way as
a stem cutting.

Ornamental Root Pieces
Used as Trunks

Potted plants which have not been root-
pruned can produce some unusual root
shapes. The more mature the plant is, the
more unusual are root shapes likely to be,
as the restraints of the pot over several
years will have caused much underground
twisting and coiling. As the plant ages, the
main root will also have matured and be
reasonably set in its gnarled shape.

The main root is easily distinguished once the soil is removed from
the unpotted plant and the roots are
washed. All secondary rooting is removed
from the plant except at the base of the
main root. Only this base tip is replanted,
the rest remains above ground to become
an interestingly shaped trunk wired or
staked into the style it already most
resembles — informal upright, coiled,
semi-cascade, cascade and bunjin being
the most accessible styles.

The stem of the original plant can be
greatly reduced in length which will
encourage the production of new shoots
ready for training into style. Initially this
plant may need some support as the root

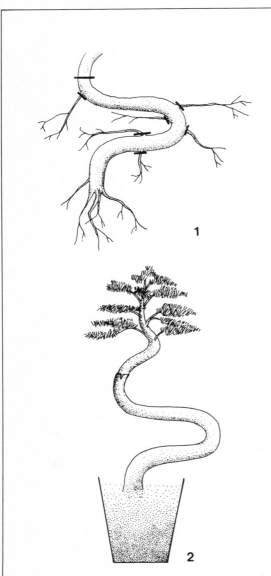

ORNAMENTAL ROOTS
USED AS TRUNKS

Ornamental root pieces can be used as trunks, fig. 1. They may retain their original stem or be grafted, fig. 2, with selected flower, fruit or foliage. Secondary roots are removed from all but the base of the cutting to leave a clean stem. At the base, these roots are retained for repotting.

will lack the necessary anchorage to stab: ise it in the pot. The newly exposed ro: should not be subjected to long periods sunlight until the bark has matured.

Exposed-root style, where an a: tractive root system is displayed, is easy produce in this way. Roots are exposed : arranged by nature or rearranged into more exciting shape with only the ti being repotted.

Unusually shaped root systems ca also be used as understocks for graftin Roots of plants that are not normal capable of propagation by root cutting c: be used as grafting understocks. Thus : almost limitless range of plant materi can be comparatively quickly presented mature-looking bonsai subjects witho the years of training necessary to establi most of the formal bonsai styles.

Grafting

The vegetative propagation of both cu tings and layers produce their own ro systems. With grafting, the cutting, scion, is united with the root, or stock, another plant. This stock — also called t understock or rootstock — may be a see ling one to two years old, root-pruned ar potted, or it may be a more mature tre Living cell tissue in between the bark ar the wood, the cambium, is the growir part of the plant. By bringing the cambiu of the stock into intimate contact with th of the scion, the union of the two parts ca be achieved. There are two simple tec niques.

Cleft Graft

With a cleft graft, the understock is c down to a convenient or desirable heig and a vertical cut is made into the ste about 3 cm long. A scion of about 10 c long is prepared by removing all but t the top two or three leaves and cutti these remaining leaves in half. The base the stem is cut into a wedge shape equal length or just slightly longer than t incision in the understock. The scion

Top: Japanese five-needle pine, *Pinus parviflora*, in a natural grouping of 11 trees.
Bottom: The splendid root system of the trident maple,
Acer buergeranum, makes it an ideal subject
for root over rock settings.

Three pots hold miniature figs each trained into proportions
appropriate for the varied sizes of the pots.

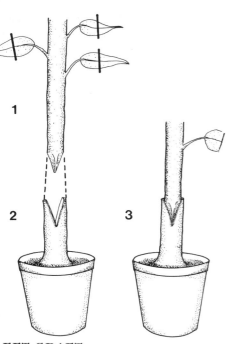

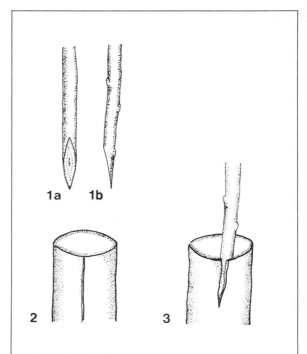

LEFT GRAFT

The scion, trimmed to three half-leaves, is cut into a wedge at its base. (Fig. 1)

The stock is cleft to a depth sufficient to take the wedge. (Fig. 2)

The scion inserted ready for tying. The efficient use of grafting tape can eliminate the use of waxes or other types of sealer. (Fig. 3)

BARK GRAFT

An incision is made in the bark of the stock about 3 cm long.(Figs 1a, 1b)

The base of the scion is cut diagonally. The cut is also 3 cm long or equal in length to the incision in the stock. (a) Front view of cut, (b) side view. (Fig. 2)

The scion is inserted under the bark ready for tying with grafting tape. (Fig. 3)

then inserted into the cleft, matching cambium to cambium, and then tied securely with grafting tape.

Bark Graft

A vertical incision about 3 cm long is made in the bark at the top of the stock. The bark is then lifted away from the wood but not removed. A scion of about 10 cm long is prepared in much the same way as for the cleft graft, except that a one-sided cut equal in length to the incision in the bark is made at the base of its stem. The scion is then inserted and both parts are tied

securely with grafting tape. This process is more easily done when the plant is growing actively, or in winter when the plant is then placed on bottom heat for three to four weeks at a temperature of about 27°C.

GENERAL CARE

Like every cultivated plant, a bonsai setting needs water, food and protection from predators and from elements that are harsher than would be found in its natural environment. Unlike other cultivated plants, most miniatures require a routine of daily care.

Water

There are no rigid rules relating to the frequency or volume of water to apply to any given bonsai. It must be controlled according to the environment, aspect, exposure to sun or wind and the season of the year. The soil must also be taken into account, its value for moisture retention, and the quantity in the pot. It is important to keep in mind that some of the miniature bonsai containers may hold only a maximum soil volume of one or two teaspoons.

Watering Methods
Water may be applied by a hand-held hose fitted with any of the accepted water-distribution nozzles to suit the bonsai grower. Watering-cans are popular, especially those of Japanese design, which give a soft, fine-spreading flow that will not damage or displace even newly planted moss. Cans are ideal for the small collection.

Dunking is an efficient watering method during hot summer months. Place the bonsai pot in a container of water filled to cover the soil and moss. Leave the bonsai in the dunking dish until air bubbles cease. Then remove it for draining and return to the display bench. By this method the soil is thoroughly saturated, so dunking can be carried out less frequently than ordinary watering. Many bonsai are harmed by excessive watering. The key word is "moist" soil.

Fertilisers

The object of bonsai is to produce a miniature tree according to the classification for size. The indiscriminate use of fertiliser could well upset this, so the quantities used should be sufficient to allow the tree to perform its normal botanical function without any excess growth. The fertiliser may be mixed with the soil or used in liquid form applied with a watering-can. There are many fertilisers on the market, so select one formulated for trees and shrubs. Slow-release fertilisers are hard to apply to an ornamental pot and are not recommended.

An excess of fertiliser will give rise to elongation of the shoot and an increase in leaf size and internodal length — the distance between leaves. This upsets the spacing of the branches, resulting in a breakdown of the very thing we are aiming for, balanced proportion of parts of the plant making up a perfect tree. Vigorous new growth initiated by the use of additional fertiliser makes more work for the bonsai grower in pruning and controlling the future miniature tree.

Traditionally the Japanese use small pieces of bamboo for applying fertiliser. The bamboo stems were hollow and about 5 cm long. They were strategically placed on the surface of the moss, say three to five to a bonsai pot 30 cm long and each hollow tube was filled with a selected fertiliser paste. With the aid of rain or watering, the liquidised fertiliser filtered through to the soil where it was absorbed by the root system.

Nowadays the Japanese have replaced the bamboo with a plastic perforated cup fitted with three prongs to keep it in place in the moss. Its slow release of fertiliser paste works in much the same way as did the bamboo.

The recommended dosage is that which is printed on the fertiliser pack.

On those occasions when the fertiliser is mixed with the bonsai potting soil, its lifespan is usually accepted as expiring after the first year of potting or repotting. Liquid fertiliser can be applied, say, every two weeks during the growing season for the second and third years or until repotting takes place.

Plant Protection

The size of a bonsai does not exclude it from attack by insects or disease. A miniature tree only a few centimetres high would make a tasty breakfast for a hungry caterpillar.

Included in the tools and equipment for bonsai culture is a specially designed pair of tweezers called "pincettes". These are for removing spiders, caterpillars, leaf-hoppers, etcetera, by those growers who do not like using their fingers. Plant-protection techniques give the bonsai grower the option to either develop and maintain a preventive spray programme using insecticides suitable for the type of insect likely to attack a given type of tree; or to critically look at each bonsai at least once a day for the presence of some sort of attack. This visual examination of the bonsai will overcome the necessity of using insecticidal sprays.

Insects are divided into two categories related to their feeding habits. The first includes the biters and chewers. These are the insects that produce physical damage to the foliage. Very few of them, if any, have any special routine — they may consume part of a leaf and move off to another; others eat whole leaves. All that is left is a portion of the petiole or stalk. Others may attack only the newer leaves. Do not forget they will eat leaf and flower buds as well as tender bark when leaves are not present.

The second type are those having sucking mouth parts. These are the crafty ones, concealing themselves for the most part on the back of the leaves or stems or buds. They stick their beaks into the cells and suck out the sap. The results of this type of feeding are not so obvious. On occasions, some distortion may take place as well as reduction in leaf size. Since the physical damage is not so obvious, these insects can go undetected for long periods and build up large populations on a single tree or branch.

The insecticides do not discriminate between chewer or sucker. Both consume the poison, but the visual inspection may miss the small sucking insects. The answer to this of course is to view the bonsai from all angles, topside and backside, even underneath the pot.

Nowadays there appears to be a distinct division amongst plant people, some being in favour and some against the use of insecticides. Bonsai growers are indeed fortunate in that their trees are capable of being handled for visual inspection and control of insects.

Assuming that the bonsai is given lots of loving care, disease is not something to be greatly worried about. The most common complaint is two forms of fungus disease. One is a white mildew, the other a sooty mould. White mildew is a restricted foliage disease attacking only a few selected trees. It appears as a white powdery patch on the upper surface of the leaf and, if not controlled, many spread to many or all of the leaves on the tree. Fungicides for its control are freely available. Sooty mould may occur on leaf or stem. It is inconspicuous in its early stages and may be confused with pollution when the upper surface of the leaf appears dirty. Badly infected trees often appear to be carrying black foliage. Once again, use a suitable fungicide to control it.

Like all these things, talking about it is useless. Get the spray and use it. Keep your trees clean. To coin a phrase, use good housekeeping in the garden.

Defoliation

Defoliation refers to a practice sometimes used in Japan where all the leaves are removed from a tree to force ahead an entirely new batch of foliage. It is suggested that the new leaves will be smaller in size and will retain a fresh spring look for the remainder of the season.

The need to defoliate may be necessitated by other reasons, the most common of which is damage to the leaves by extreme heat or the ravages of insects. It is necessary where physical damage is so obvious that the tree must be put out of the display area.

Leaf-pruning or defoliation of deciduous trees appears to be a very desirable bonsai technique, but was little practised by the early bonsai growers in the west.

In temperate regions it is fraught with danger and could lead to the death of a tree. However, there are benefits which could outweigh the risk. Japanese maples in particular are somewhat heat-tender in the average hot summer of temperate zones. Leaf-burning is fairly common and this in turn spoils the whole autumn scene. The much-awaited autumn colour is non-existent and so it is tempting to defoliate.

Most of the maples are in full leaf by the end of the first four weeks of spring, and by summer are starting to show signs of wear and tear. The tips of the lobes are the first to brown off, followed by the margins, and then the blade of the leaf has that dried look. Under these conditions, it might even be worthwhile to leaf-prune anyway, just to get a new batch of leaves regardless of what other benefits may accrue. In theory, leaf-pruning sounds very practical. In practice, it may require a lot of finger-crossing. We can assume that new buds will form or the buds already forming for next year's growth will burst forth and produce an entirely new batch of leaves in about four weeks from pruning. This means that the new foliage will appear by the last month of summer. This time is usually the hottest and will not favour the delicate new maple leaves. A temperature of 40°C or more with hot dry winds will cook the leaves and this will probably be the end of the maple.

Tools and Equipment

Many tools of Japanese origin for working on bonsai are now available outside Japan. Some are of unique design. All of them are for specific tasks. Basic tools and other equipment required depend on the scope of the work and the skills and desires of the grower.

Tools needed can range from simple tool set of four or five pieces to complicated assembly of more than 4 items. Beginners obviously may not wis to purchase expensive equipment substitutes can be found amongst ordina garden tools.

The most important tools for bons are as follows:

Scissors Long-handled leaf- and twi pruners are used for light pruning control the height and shape of the trur and branches. They are far superior to th usual heavily constructed garden sec teurs and allow access into compact, har to-get-at spots. They need to be kept clea and sharp for efficient use.

Scissors (heavy-duty cutters) They a for use in root-pruning and are th standard for most root work. The cuttir edges will blunt quickly when they a used in gritty, sandy soil. They should cleaned after each operation, dried ar then wiped or sprayed with rust-resistir oils before being put back into the to box. This tool is commonly referred to root-pruning shears.

Potting Sticks Potting sticks can vary size according to the work, from miniatu bonsai to larger bonsai. Steel knittir needles, or meat skewers are ideal. The main use is to remove soil from the ro ball to allow easy root-pruning. A host other uses will be found for them. O some occasions, the Japanese use cho sticks (two at a time, often a difficult tas for westerners).

Cultivator This tool has at one end three-pronged fork, bent at right angles the handle, and at the other end a mini ture trowel, used for the same purpose the pincettes (see below). The forked en is for the removal of soil and straightenir out the roots from the root ball whe repotting. It is far more efficient than th potting sticks when working on large bonsai.

General-purpose Knife Classified as bootmaker's knife, this is a very usef implement in general repotting work. can be used for running around the insi of the pot where the soil and roots meet

sist in the easy removal of plant from
ot. It is also useful for taking off moss
om the soil surface, for working the
oss ready for remossing after repotting,
d for general cutting duties. It is not
tended to be a super-sharp knife.

ncettes One end is a miniature trowel
ed for shaping and smoothing the soil
ter repotting in an ornamental pot. The
owel is also used for working the moss
d firming it to the soil.

The other end is a pair of tweezers
ed for the removal of the sharp needle-
e leaves of the junipers and other
nifers. It is also useful for the removal
spiders, insects and leaves and for
eding.

anch-cutters or Concave Cutters These
e designed for the complete removal of
anches and are far more efficient than
y other cutting instrument. In one cut,
e selected branch is separated, leaving a
at concave depression. This allows for
ick healing without obvious scars.

This is an expensive piece of equip-
ent and should be used only for what it is
tended. It could then be expected to last
lifetime. After use, wipe the cutting
ges, oil and stow it away.

il Scoops It has taken a long time to
hieve some sort of dignity in horticultural
rsuits! No longer do we grab a handful
soil and throw it into a pot! Soil scoops
ansfer the soil to the bonsai pot.

hisk Made of coconut fibre, this is
metimes referred to as a mossing brush.
is used for smoothing the soil while
potting, sweeping away excess soil, and
r cleaning the mossed surface of the
namental pots. The texture of the fibre
ay vary. The softer ones should be
lected for moss sweeping so that there
little or no danger of disturbing even
wly applied moss.

ditional Tools and Equipment Large
ot-cutter; large branch-cutter or concave
tter; small branch-cutter; wire-cutter;
afting knife, Japanese design; grafting
ife, European; sharpening stones under
afting knives; hand-carving tools (six);
rk remover; hooked knife; steel chisels
ve); squeeze scissors; copper wire.

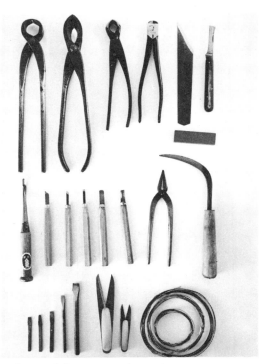

Some of the many tools used in bonsai work.

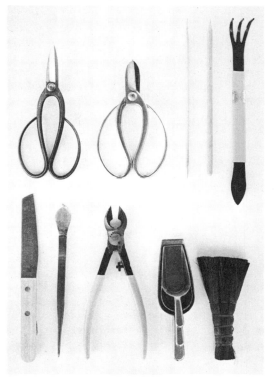

GARDEN AND HOME SETTINGS

In this book we have been discussing bonsai for the home and garden. Bonsai can be displayed equally well indoors or out, but it must be remembered that the trees and shrubs used for training as bonsai specimens are normally outdoor plants. Therefore, display indoors should be restricted to short periods of time from one to two days, and then only where there is no air-conditioning or high-temperature heating within the room. But just as important, many of the trees chosen for bonsai may not suit a particular garden. For example, it may be a tropical plant expected to survive in a frost-prone area. Therefore, the bonsai outdoors must also be protected. The elements that can cause most alarm in any type of bonsai's weather pattern are sun, wind, rainfall, extremes of temperature and even air pollution.

Where to Place Bonsai

The ideal "room" of the house is the outdoor living area, the covered terrace, pergola or open verandah. Also popular is the shade house structure designed to protect against the midday sun and any prevailing winds of a drying nature. Modern shade cloth is an efficient agent against both problems. There are different textures available, and its capacity to provide shade is governed by the closeness of the weave. The shade cloth allows water penetration and during thunderstorms, heavy rain is broken up, coming through like a Scotch mist.

Bonsai in the Garden

If we take Japan as the standard where the summer temperature would rarely exceed 35°C, the bonsai are fully exposed, a border of trees or perhaps an ornamental bamboo fence providing protection from the wind. Extra protection is provided during the typhoon season when most bonsai growers tie their trees to their display benches in preparation for the extremely strong winds.

In wintertime, some protection can be given against frost damage. The Japanese often use a wooden frame erected over the bench to support a roof and three sides of straw matting with the south side usually exposed. Individual trees may also be kept in box-like structures, once again with one side open. The tree can be turned round periodically within the box. Snow or rain entering or blowing into the shelter does no harm — frost is the enemy. In extreme cold where the temperature is below freezing, the shelters are closed in on four sides. Circulation of air is important and for this reason the shelter sheds are made of boards rather than glass or corrugated iron.

Watering is carried out by hand using long-spouted watering-cans fitted with a fine rose. Every pot receives individual care. A supply of pure water is usually contained in large ornamental ceramic pots as much as 1 m in diameter. The water is exposed to the air for about 24 hours before use. Chlorinated water direct from the tap is rarely used. On occasions, goldfish may be kept in the ornamental bowls.

In warmer zones where summer temperatures may exceed 38°C and thunderstorms abound, semi-shade is ideal. This is best provided by a permanent shelter with stands, tables or benches designed to fit the space, and a cover of shade cloth of 50 per cent to 72 per cent density.

The roof height does not appear to be of great importance in the variation of the shade density. It is more likely to be related to design and convenience for working in the shelter area. Wind protection can be achieved by using shade cloth as side walls.

A slightly sloping roof is preferable as this eliminates pockets of rainwater dripping into the pots which can damage the moss and splash out the soil.

Bonsai should not be placed directly on the ground. Bricks, concrete or timber

n be used as a base. Dog owners should
ovide some protection.

Birds can be a cause of damage
om stealing the moss for nesting pur-
ses to breaking small branches. On the
her hand, the insectivorous birds should
: encouraged and a permanent drinking
wl could be installed.

mmer Care of Miniature Bonsai

e average miniature bonsai pot has a
pacity of about one tablespoon of soil.
e moisture content of such a small
antity of soil will evaporate rapidly on a
t day. To conserve the moisture, some
otection will be necessary. This may
ke the form of overhead shade using
ade cloth or a plastic woven mesh sus-
nded above the bench. The pots can be
pt cool by burying them in soil or sand.
box or tray deep enough to take the
epest miniature bonsai pot is used. The
ts are placed in the tray, leaving a space
tween each pot. Dry, clean sand is then
ured in, filling the tray to the top
thout spilling over the moss in the
nsai pots.

niature bonsai placed in a sand tray during
mmer to aid in the conservation of moisture in the
s.

How to Display and Position Outside

Traditional display is on table-height benches, with the length and width to suit the
available space. Individual trees can be
staged on small tables which in turn are
also suitable for a number of miniatures.
On rare occasions, taller stands may be
used, mostly towards or at the back of the
display. The trees on fixed benches are
periodically turned to give each side of the
plant adequate light or sunshine.

The stands can be placed to draw
attention to a selected point of interest in
the garden or may become the main point
of interest themselves, especially in
entrance ways.

If a number of bonsai are being
displayed on a long table or bench, place
them in a single row, clear of each other.
Where individual trees are on tall stands,
they should be tied on to prevent acciden-
tal knocking-off. Miniature bonsai are
placed to give an eye-appealing display.

The use of glasshouses has, up until
this time, been restricted to winter care
for the semi- and tropical plants. For
species of figs which have failed to survive
the short cold period (*F. benjamina* is one
in particular which is very sensitive to
cold), it may be of interest to note that the
switch from outside to the glasshouse does
not necessarily mean that new growth is
induced, even when the tree is placed on a
hot bench with a temperature of 24°C, but
it can save a plant. Glasshouses do not
play a major role in bonsai culture.

Exhibiting

When it is anticipated that a tree may be
entered in an exhibition, the trunk may be
scrubbed. This includes the exposed roots.
The moss can be renewed if it is not looking its best and the pot itself carefully
wiped free of mud or dirt.

Bonsai in the Home

The interior decoration of the western house
does not lend itself to displaying as it is

done in Japan. Whilst it may be difficult to duplicate a traditional setting, it is possible to improvise to achieve a traditional effect. To look its best, good bonsai display should have no competition from other displays, such as a bowl of flowers or a dominating picture, or brightly coloured objects.

The traditional display is arranged in an alcove (*tokonoma* in Japan) situated in the principal room of the house, and forms part of the only decoration in the room. A bonsai is never displayed alone in the alcove. It is always accompanied by a hanging scroll and a second smaller bonsai or an ornament. This second bonsai should contrast with the first. For example, a single tree offset by a small herb or a rock planting. Often a piece of carving or a fine rock is substituted for the second bonsai. The principal bonsai always stands on some form of base. If a number of miniature bonsai are used instead of a single tree, they are displayed on a tiered stand. In the western house, a table placed in a selected part of the room can be used, and it should be big enough to accommodate both the principal and second bonsai, or other suitable decoration. The background should be uniform and subdued to highlight the shape of the principal tree. A number of miniature bonsai could be substituted on the same table.

Existing furniture can also be used to good effect, and when the background clashes with the proposed setting, a plain white screen or even a white curtain can serve.

Flat- and unit-dwellers need not be left out. Some of the house plants, especially the figs, can be selected and trained, and will survive indoor life as they normally would given their usual requirements for light and care.

Balconies are useful for fresh air and possibly rain or at least for a good washing-down every couple of weeks or so during the summer. Where there are no balconies, the bonsai can be taken downstairs to an open space and treated to a hosing-down and, if it is safe to do so, eve left out in the rain.

The bonsai can be placed in positio for the arrival of visitors or purely for th benefit of the owner. Bonsai are fc looking at and their ornamental value is c primary importance.

Bonsai Pots

There are some simple guidelines lai down for the selection of pots. Before w discuss them, it must be stressed that th most important procedure is to select an train the tree, then think about the pot.

Pot Shapes

The basic shapes are square, round, ov; and rectangular. Variations occur, such ; five-sided or six-sided pots, up to many sided. Some are shaped like the petals of flower.

Tall square, shallow square, squar pots with sharp corners, square pots wit rounded corners, straight sides, slopin sides, square pots incurved at the to; square pots flared at the top — all ar suitable. There are long, narrow oval pot; wide oval pots and narrow rectangular t almost square pots.

Simple feet, ornamental feet, glaze pots, unglazed — there is a tremendou range to select from, and this variet should satisfy every taste.

The Japanese tell us that what th frame is to the picture, the pot is to th bonsai.

Pot Colours

Pot colours are somewhat limited to brow and red (terracotta), grey-green and ve1 earthy colours. In the glazed pots, blue white and celedon (green) with an oc casional mottled light brown to buff anc on very rare occasions, a black glaze ar available.

Some brighter colour glazes are o; the pots used for miniatures. Som feature simple landscape designs, givin the pot a more Chinese effect.

There is keen competition today between the pottery factories and the individual potters. They vie for superior and original designs and for colour and distribution of colour in both glazed and unglazed pots.

Rules for Selecting a Pot

Divide all trees into two groups:
1. deciduous;
2. evergreen.

The deciduous trees traditionally go into blue, green or white pots. The evergreens go into brown, red and grey pots.

The trees may now be divided into:
1. ornamental foliage;
2. flowering trees;
3. fruiting trees.

1. Ornamental Foliage This applies to both groups, deciduous and evergreen. It may relate to unusual shape, colour or surface texture. For example, an attractive glossy surface may look well in a blue or green pot, red leaves contrast in a white pot, and yellow autumn leaves in a blue pot.

2. Flowering Trees Most colours respond well to blue or green pots, except red flowers which are almost invariably grown in white pots. All of them will look pleasant in the earthy brown pots. Many bonsai camellias and azaleas are seen in brown pots.

3. Fruiting Trees Crabapples, berry fruits, citrus, apricots and plums are enhanced in coloured pots. The red-fruited tree is traditionally grown in a white pot; citrus and persimmon are grown in blue. Many bonsai growers choose pots to suit personal taste and disregard the guidelines. Most of the time they make a good choice. If in doubt, settle for an earthy colour.

The Size of the Pot and its Proportion to the Tree

The Japanese remind us that the size of the pot must be related to the tree and that the proportion between the two is import-
ant, but no guidelines are given as to what the proportion is. Nowadays it is generally accepted that the height of the tree can be one and a half times the length of the pot. It is surprising how quickly one becomes accustomed to the proportion. Anything less is immediately obviously overpotted, that is, the pot is too big for the tree. On the other hand, where the tree is greater than the suggested proportion, it may still appear a good combination of tree and pot. The answer may be for the bonsai grower to measure the tree or take the tree along when going to purchase the pot.

Bonsai pots and one of the many styles of stand used for display indoors.

BONSAI CALENDAR

 It is important to make a daily check on your bonsai collection to ensure each plant's needs are catered for and that there are no pests munching or sucking. In addition to this, there is an annual cycle of care which is outlined in the following calendar.

As it would be impossible to write a concise calendar which covered the many different climatic zones wherein bonsai is practised, the times given for flowering, pruning, potting, etcetera, have a bias towards the temperate regions with which I am most familiar. I have generally indicated where differences will occur, but gardeners in hot or very cold climates will sometimes need to adjust the times a month to six weeks either way, depending on their particular area.

Summer – First Month

The temperature this month could range from 35°C to 38°C in temperate and sub-tropical zones. Even in colder climate zones, some extra protection of bonsai plants will be necessary.

Those plants from cold-climate countries accepted as heat-tender should now be given the favoured spots – the coolest and shadiest. They may also need favoured treatment on very hot days. In cold-climate zones, watering may be required only every two days, but in hotter zones daily watering will almost always be necessary. For bonsai growers planning to be away from home during the holiday season, help should be organised for this period. On occasions of prolonged hot, dry conditions, dunking is recommended as an alternative watering method. Miniature bonsai may require additional protection with full shade most of the day rather than repeated excessive applications of water.

This month is recognised as the best time for propagating by cuttings. A whole range of bonsai plant material can be successfully reproduced by this method.

This is a very active period for insects. The spray programme begun in spring can be continued or frequent visual examinations of each tree can be made.

In cold-climate zones, late-flowering *satsuki* azaleas will have finished flowering and can be repotted, but most other repotting will now wait for the autumn months.

Summer – Second Month

Hot weather restricts work on the trees. The main concern is for the safety of the trees and protection of the foliage against burning. Some growers insist on keeping their bonsai fully exposed on benches, as is the custom in Japan. It is a dangerous practice in the warmer climates, since the depth of soil in a shallow pot must dry very quickly when the temperatures soar. This leads to leaf-burning and an unsightly tree for the remainder of the year.

Under heatwave conditions, bonsai can be misted using a suitable hose fitting at intervals during the day. It has a cooling effect on the immediate environment and is much better than applying copious quantities of water directly on the soil.

Any trees with wire still intact will need close attention against the wire biting into the wood, leaving a scar or series of scars which will be visible for many years. Remove wire as necessary.

A good month to take cuttings for propagation.

Continue plant protection against pest and diseases.

Summer – Third Month

High summer temperatures have the effect of reducing or stopping growth. Some years are hot and dry, but in some areas this may be the month of tropical cyclones or their effects. Tropical downpours often initiate new growth and tender new shoots are exposed to high temperatures. Many of the hardy trees tolerate such conditions, but maples, cherries, crabapples, hornbeam and beech are trees to watch.

Where weather patterns are more
[st]able some wiring can be started this
[m]onth on spring shoots which are starting
[to] mature. After about 12 weeks growth,
[th]e shoots are classified as semi-
[ha]rdwood.

This is a peak period for insects —
[th]is month may give rise to a new batch of
[ca]terpillars. They start to feed as soon as
[ha]tched and are almost invisible to the
[na]ked eye. Resting, they may assume atti-
[tu]des of disguise, and cryptic colouration
[m]atching leaves, twigs or even mature
[wo]od. Some of them may rest along the
[m]idrib on the underside of the leaf. In all,
[th]ey are very difficult to detect. Those who
[us]e insecticides should continue their
[sp]raying programme at intervals till the
[en]d of autumn.

Seedlings of this year's vintage not
[ye]t potted may still be pricked out, root-
[pr]uned and potted on. Established rooted
[cu]ttings may also be root-pruned and
[po]tted. Protect them from the heat until
[th]ey are established in their new pots.

Cuttings are still a possibility for
[pr]opagation this month.

[A]utumn — First Month

[Th]e first month of autumn can still
[pr]oduce some high temperatures. Keep an
[ey]e on the weather map and be prepared.

One can assume that the growing
[se]ason for most plants has almost come to
[a] halt. The fertilisers can be put away. In a
[fe]w weeks, leaf fall will commence.

Now is the time for most activities
[to] begin. Those wayward branches that
[fa]iled to respond to last year's wiring can
[be] rewired and positioned. New shoots
[pr]oduced in the season are maturing and
[sh]ould be wired, shaped and placed to the
[be]st advantage. Well-established seed-
[lin]gs can also have their first wiring and
[sh]aping.

Some pruning may take place, es-
[pe]cially on those shoots boosted by heavy
[ra]in or fertiliser that appear to upset the
[ba]lance of the tree. Cut them to suit the
[si]ze and shape of the bonsai.

In cold-climate zones, repotting may
commence this month but do not expose
plants so treated to the sun if a hot spell is
forecast.

Aphids usually appear in large
numbers this month. Watch flower buds
and the terminal ends of this season's
shoots. Inspect the undersides of the
leaves.

Those courageous enough may start
their repotting routine. The hardy evergreens like *Camellia sasanqua* and *C.
japonica*, *Ficus macrophylla* and *F.
rubiginosa*, rhododendrons and azaleas,
the hardy conifers and many Australian
native trees will respond quite well.
After-care is most important.

Layers can be checked for root
development. If it is adequate, they can be
detached from the parent and potted on.
Harvesting of seed can commence.

Autumn — Second Month

This is a beautiful time of year. Towards
the end of the month, colourful mature
fruit and berries are seen as well as a
mixture of autumn coloured leaves.

Those deciduous trees capable of
producing autumn colour should now be
placed in full sun in an effort to bring on
attractive colours.

Assuming one's favourite Japanese
maple has been in full shade during hot
summer months and is not suffering any
burning on the margin of the leaves, this
exposure to the sun at this time will
harden off the growth and produce
excellent colour during late autumn and
early winter.

General repotting may now begin in
earnest in warm zones and is completed in
cold-climate zones. Deciduous trees,
especially those looking the worse for
wear after the summer heat, may safely be
defoliated as part of the repotting routine.
From autumn on, there is no restriction on
repotting evergreen or deciduous, flowering or fruiting, trees with broad leaves,
trees with needle-like leaves, young trees,

old trees, trees in pots, trees taken out of the garden, this year's seedlings or this year's cuttings. This is the time.

Wiring can be continued.

Do not relax the vigilance on insect pests.

Seed collection may still be possible this month.

Autumn — Third Month

The ornamental containers may be showing soil splashes and stains from the summer watering, storms, dust-laden winds and other causes. It is a good time for a clean-up and pot-washing. Some exhibitors at bonsai shows display trees in unclean containers and obviously fail to appreciate the full aesthetic pleasure of bonsai growing where the relationship of the pot and plant is so important.

A good time to survey the year's work, especially the deciduous trees which, bare of leaves, will show the shape and position of all the branches. Are any changes to be made? These could be recorded as a reminder for future shaping.

This is the ideal month for collecting moss. The cooler weather and some autumn rain rapidly bring out the moss in good condition. Look on the shady side of fences, buildings and the shady side of rocks in the wild. It occurs in many places, probably right in your own garden. Select a similar place to store the collected moss until it is required for use, and keep it moist.

Repotting can continue in warmer zones while in very cold areas it will be necessary to keep a lookout for early frosts and prepare for winter care.

Trees requiring some winter protection can now be placed in favoured spots.

Winter — First Month

In the very cold areas, it is time to "batten down" or stow away plants in cold frames,
sheds or glasshouses. Some interio heating is acceptable on occasions, bu overheating could cause new shoots t emerge. Overnight shelters may be ad equate as frost protection in some areas

In the southern hemisphere this ca be a variable month, sometimes wet an cold, and at other times dry and mild. I can bring good working weather when it i possible to continue potting and mossing

Watering will be restricted but d not allow bonsai to dry out.

If the weather is fine, display area can be cleaned down and moss can b checked for any weed growth. There ar only a few weeks to go until the sprin display of bursting buds for both leaf an flower growth.

During mild winters, some insect like grasshoppers, stick insects, katydid and caterpillars are still active, even o deciduous trees. If there are no leaves t eat, they will consume the buds and bark together with the conducting tissue unde neath the bark.

Repotting is possible except in ver cold areas where glasshouse condition would be necessary for this work.

Winter — Second Month

Like the previous month, this is a period o little activity. This does not mean that th bonsai should be ignored. Check pots moss, moisture content of the soil and th foliage of the evergreen trees. Water onl when necessary.

Now is a good time to think abou provision of shade and shelter for th hotter months to follow.

Construction of shade house should be completed without delay, a even late winter can produce unseasonabl high temperatures and drying winds ar commonplace.

This is an excellent time for diggin plants from the garden. Root-prune then and place in training pots ready for th first pruning and training. This applies t both evergreen and deciduous trees.

In warmer areas, the first winter-flowering tree, the Japanese apricot, should be reaching its peak this month; followed by the early-flowering Taiwan cherry, *Prunus campanulata*, with its red bells; then come the winter peaches and plums. These can be root-pruned and repotted after flowering.

Winter — Third Month

This is the ideal month for seed-sowing and the propagation of future bonsai plants by the use of seed.

Check all wired plants at the first sign of bud swell. Take off wire by cutting with the special wire-cutters or by carefully unwinding it to avoid damage and loss of buds.

A fertiliser programme can be started in warmer zones for those trees not repotted this year.

Repotting should be completed at or just before bud swell. Some deciduous trees will be active before the end of this month. The Japanese and trident maples, if mature enough, will flower before the leaves; some of the early crabapples have also been recorded in flower this month.

Winter should never be a dull period. Camellias, magnolias, rhododendrons and azaleas can all be found in flower before spring in warmer climates, while the Japanese apricot, Taiwan cherry, flowering peaches and plums will be gracing gardens now in colder areas. All can be root-pruned and repotted after flowering.

Any sign of leaf-bud swelling is the signal to bring out those deciduous trees which are early-growing.

Some propagation may be undertaken this month — grafting and preparation for layering. Seed-sowing can also commence. Scions for grafting can be collected, washed in a mild solution of disinfectant, placed in plastic bags and stored in the refrigerator until required for spring grafting.

Spring — First Month

If bonsai have been stored over winter, they can now be brought out into the open. In some areas, maples and a few other deciduous trees are now running riot, from swelling buds to rapidly growing shoots. This is the most exciting time of the year. Not only is it beautiful, but it is also an active period.

At this early stage some pruning may take place on newly emerging shoots which are soft and succulent. These can be removed with the thumb and finger rather than with a cutting instrument. The advantage of pinching out tips is an almost invisible scar at the point of pruning. During this rapid growth period, a careful watch should be maintained on those branches which may still carry copper wire. Remove as necessary.

Seed-sowing can continue this month. As soon as the seedlings are big enough to be handled with the fingertips, they can be removed, root-pruned and potted on. Propagation of new plants by layering can start this month.

Insect activity also becomes more noticeable. Spraying for control may begin now. Read the instructions on the container and follow as directed.

The watering programme should be adjusted to meet the increasing temperatures and more active growth. The tender new leaves will suffer if watering is neglected on warmer days. A fertiliser programme can begin in colder zones and should be continued in warmer zones on all but plants repotted this year.

Grafting of most deciduous trees can take place this month.

Spring — Second Month

This is the month of care against unexpected heat that can damage the tender new leaves; against dry weather cracking and breaking up the moss which was applied late; and against dehydration of the soil in the shallow pots, especially the miniature bonsai which should be given the extra protection of shade and kept cool by burying the pots in a tray of soil.

By this time, most trees will be approaching their peak of growth. Long, lush shoots are commonplace. These may be reduced back to two or three buds as required, or they may be left awhile to mature a little more. Check grafted plants.

If not already done, it is time to revise watering programmes for more frequent applications and to take a more critical look at your trees for evidence of insect attack. Fertilising programmes should continue.

Check grafted plants and remove any new shoots arising below the point of grafting. Layers can also be inspected.

Spring — Third Month

The late-flowering azaleas, mostly those classified as *satsuki*, will charm us with their blossom from now until early summer. The early spring-flowering types, the *kurume* and *indicas*, by this time have made their first growth and may need some pruning, preferably with the fingers.

By the end of spring, many trees have completed their annual growth. Pruning for control of size as well as shape may continue as required.

Do not forget the wiring. Perhaps concealed by the new spring growth, it should be carefully checked now.

Continue the fertiliser programme.

Keep a watchful eye against insect attack, act promptly and, in areas plagued by the pest, do not forget that many ornamental fruiting trees may, in some areas, be subject to attack by fruit-fly.

Some cuttings can be collected at this time from plants that have flowered in late winter and early spring.

A SELECT LIST OF PLANTS SUITABLE FOR BONSAI

When selecting trees, bonsai growers may be influenced by personal likes and dislikes, books and magazines, or by attending bonsai exhibitions. Bonsai's eastern origins perhaps exert more pressure than any other source and many of the traditional Japanese trees are suitable, even for temperate climates, and are available in bonsai nurseries.

Another particular consideration when choosing plants for bonsai can be the size of their leaves, flowers and fruit. Eye-pleasing proportions being so critical to good bonsai, it is understandably tempting, when learning the art, to think small. However, in practice, bonsai work places few such restrictions on choice. For example, while a flower the size of the average *Camellia japonica* would certainly look out of place on a miniature bonsai, it would be beautifully in proportion as a medium or large bonsai. Persimmon, citrus and Chinese quince, which all produce large fruit, are grown frequently in Japan for bonsai. However, the number of pieces of fruit allowed to remain is limited to perhaps three, which are stragically placed in the form of a triangle with one fruit towards the apex of the tree. Some trees will adjust their leaf size to the environment in which they grow — the large-leafed Moreton Bay fig is an example. On the bonsai plant, fig leaves are reduced in size and often well in proportion. *Kurume* azaleas with naturally small flowers are extremely popular bonsai subjects. Yet the standard azalea used in Japan for bonsai is the *satsuki* which bears flowers up to 10 cm in diameter.

There is thus little restriction in the range of plant material suitable for bonsai and readers might find particular pleasure in working with flora native to their area. Not only will it be climatically suitable, but there is fascination in having a full-scale subject available for comparison with your bonsai — an aged giant oak, for example, and a miniature growing in its shelter and quite comfortable in a 5 cm pot.

Serious workers with such material should keep accurate records of behaviour, response to root- and top-pruning, effects of drought, extreme temperature and excess rainfall. There is little known about the bonsai culture of trees other than those native to the East, so this information will be valuable for future work.

AZALEA
See Rhododendron

BANKSIA
Banksia serrata
An Australian evergreen tree which, when mature, has the appearance of an ancient

bonsai. The trunk, often gnarled, twisted and covered with a rough-looking bark, adds to this illusion. It is best known for its cream to yellow honey-laden flowers which occur as vertical spikes shaped like large bottlebrushes and about 15 cm long and often 9 cm wide. The leaves are tough and leathery with a very distinctive toothed margin.

Banksia serrata is suitable for a range of bonsai styles — formal, informal, slanting, multi-trunks and raft. As a young tree in training, the base swells rapidly, giving the perfect shape, tapering toward the top.

Potting and repotting are possible most months of the year in temperate zones, except when the plant is in active growth. This species responds well to root-pruning at two to three-year intervals.

Wiring is done in late summer towards or at the end of the growing season, and the plant needs protection from extreme cold.

Propagation is by seed which are contained in woody follicles (cob). These should be collected in autumn and stored in a warm, dry place to assist in the release of the seed. Sow in a standard seed mix and keep warm. Flowers could be expected from six to 10 years from seed-grown plants. They often appear grossly out of proportion with the plant.

BOX, JAPANESE
Buxus microphylla var. *japonica*

A dwarf evergreen shrub with sm leaves, occurring in an opposite arrang ment. Whilst it has many potential styl box is most popular for miniature work. recent years, an American cultivar, *Bux microphylla* "Kingsville" has been provi popular for miniature work.

It is an extremely slow-growing tr with mature leaves measuring only 8 m by 5 mm. These are dark green and glos and always attractive-looking.

Pruning is the main method shaping box, as it is difficult to apply w to the tiny branches. Box is best shap into a compact, rounded head and can pruned twice during the growing seasor

Potting can be carried out in ma months of the year — in fact, whenever t plant is not in active growth.

Propagation is easy from cuttin

Trident maple, *Acer buergeranum*, exposed root style.

An informal upright style Japanese maple, *Acer palmatum*,
showing colourful new spring foliage, and an unusual miniature bonsai
using a native Australian orchid and fern.

A coiled style English hawthorn, *Crataegus laevigata*, decorates a tiled entry path.

Top: Miniature informal upright style Japanese maple
in a handmade pot no more than 4cm in diameter.

Bottom: Bonsai will thrive indoors if proper attention is given
to their usual requirements for light and care.

LUEBERRY ASH
laeocarpus reticulatus

n Australian native which is almost
mpletely neglected as a garden tree. As
rainforest tree, it is tall and straight. In
e sandstone areas of the coastal fringes,
is irregular to dwarf, often with multiple
unks, suggesting its uses for bonsai from
rmal upright to group plantings to clump
yles.

The flowers in clusters are funnel-
rm, like tiny wedding bells with a
inged margin, white in colour. More
ectacular is the pink-flowered form. The
uit, about pea size, is a beautiful blue
d may be still on the tree at next year's
owering.

Blueberry ash would need some
nter protection in cold zones.

In the temperate climates, pruning
possible many months of the year as is
potting.

Propagation is from seed or cutting.
Fruit harvested and cleaned in
nter can be soaked in warm water.
ermination may be as low as five per
nt. But leave ungerminated seed in the
t for one more year.

BEECH, JAPANESE
Fagus crenata

A popular and outstanding bonsai specimen in Japan, the white beech is grown in
many different styles and is seen mostly in
winter with the dead leaves still attached
to the tree. Exhibition trees are scrubbed
to emphasise the white bark. Group plantings and clump styles are very popular.

The European beech, *F. sylvatica*, in
its many varieties and cultivars is more
freely available than the Japanese and is
more suitable to the colder zones.

Potting in spring in cold climates
will generally be required every two years.

Propagation is mostly by seed,
except for cultivars. Trees grown in
temperate zones produce little, if any,
viable seed, therefore seed would be
imported from colder zones. Sow seed in
spring after stratification.

Camellia sasanqua, twin-trunk style.

CAMELLIA
Camellia

There is a large range of these ornamental trees and shrubs which are usually considered to have superior foliage for colour, shape and gloss. Some opinion suggests that the splendour of their flowers places the camellias amongst the top three flowering plants in the world.

Those of Japanese origin are popular and traditional bonsai subjects, yet their cultivation is limited to one particular area in the south island of Kyushu known as Kumamoto. It is here that a traditional camellia, the higo camellia, is cherished particularly.

In the late 1950s little was known about camellia bonsai in the western world and it was assumed that the *sasanqua* camellia, having smaller flowers, would be the natural choice for such work. It was a decade later when we first heard about the higo camellia and its popularity in Japan.

My Japanese friends say double flowers are vulgar and all bonsai camellias are single-flower forms. This means that the flower consists of a single row of petals with a group of decorative stamens in the centre.

Camellias are usually shaped into the informal upright style. On rare occasions they may be seen in slanting-trunk or semi-cascade styles.

Camellia sasanqua

The *sasanqua*, usually classified as a sma[ll] tree, may more often appear as a mul[ti-] trunk tree or shrub, depending on t[he] method of propagation. If it is grown fro[m] seed, it usually produces a single trun[k] but if grown from a cutting, it is genera[lly] possible to present the resulting tree as [a] plant with two or more trunks.

Leaves of *sasanqua* vary in shape a[nd] size up to about 8 cm long and 4 cm wid[e.] This size often is reduced with the m[a-] turity of the bonsai. They are thus ve[ry] useful subjects for miniatures.

The flowers, usually found in t[he] upper axils of the leaves, vary from one [to] a few with a colour range of white, pink[,] red and cerise. Single-flower forms wou[ld] be ideal and size is of no great importanc[e.] It is interesting to note that the Japanes[e] master Nakamura was quite happy [to] produce just one flower on each of h[is] miniature *sasanqua*.

Propagation may be done by cutti[ng] or grafting. Seedlings may take six [or] more years to flower. On one occasio[n a] flower was recorded in three years. See[d] capsules can be collected when rip[e,] usually when brown in colour. The see[d is] extracted by cutting the capsule open, [then] sown or stored in a dry place until sprin[g.]

n occasions, early sowing and placing the
ed pot on a hot bench can speed up
rmination.

mellia japonica
date, very little interest has been shown
the use of Camellia japonica in bonsai,
t it is a suitable subject if single-flower
rieties are available. As a garden plant,
is classified as a small evergreen tree
th very attractive glossy foliage about 10
1 long and 3 to 4 cm wide, producing
ant leaves on rare occasions. Flowers
ry in size from about 7 cm in diameter to
cm, in a range of colours from white,
nks and reds to an odd so-called yellow.

These should be wired in late
mmer to early autumn and pruned in
d-spring. Later pruning could stop
wer production since the flower bud is
oduced on that season's growth.

Potting and root-pruning can be
fected at any time when the plant is not
owing.

Propagation is mostly by cutting in
d- to late summer. Grafting is also
ssible.

mellia reticulata
much larger camellia than the previous
o, the reticulata originated in China.
ese are the super-flowered camellias,
me bearing blooms as large as dinner

plates. Flower size has been recorded up
to 20 cm.

The wild *reticulata*, with an exquis-
ite single flower which is two-toned white
and pink up to about 8 cm in diameter,
would be the ideal choice for bonsai work.
The tree itself is a loose, open-branched
structure, but it is quite easily controlled.
Some of the hybrids with smaller single
flowers are all potential bonsai subjects.

Wiring should be effected in late
summer and pruning is carried out in
spring. Potting and root-pruning is possible for many months of the year when the
plant is not actively growing.

Small-flowered species

New species of *Camellia* were introduced
from the East in the 1940s and were
beautifully in proportion for bonsai work.
These included *C. cuspidata* with white
flowers and narrow, elliptical-shaped
leaves no larger than 5 to 6 cm; *C.
lutchuensis* with flowers that open from a
pink but develop into white flowers; and *C.
rosaeflora* which, as its name implies, has
rose-like flowers. Other species have
small, single white flowers from 1.5 to 3
cm in diameter and of typical camellia
shape.

The small-flowered species are
suitable for informal upright, slanting,
semi-cascade and twin-trunk styles.

Pruning, wiring and repotting is as
for other camellias.

Propagation is by seed and seedlings can produce flower in about five
years, by which time an attractive shape
can be achieved and some slight variations
could be expected in flower size and
colour. These species are also easy to grow
from semi-hardwood cuttings taken in
summer and are equally responsive to
grafting.

Higo camellia

The origin of the higo camellia is recorded
as the product of a breeding programme
between the well-known *C. japonica* and a
little-known snow camellia, *C. rusticana*,
which is found in a restricted area of
north-western Japan. The most notable

feature of this camellia is the distinctive shape of its flower which is single-petalled, filled with stamens and much like apricot blossom. It occurs in colours ranging from white, pink, crimson, scarlet and even gold-patterned. This is a particular favourite in Japanese bonsai work with camellias.

The technique of producing bonsai from the higo camellia is very different from other bonsai forms. Firstly, it is usually grafted onto old and gnarled stocks which are probably 10 cm or more in diameter. There is enormous advantage in using these pre-shaped stocks which, under ordinary bonsai techniques, would take half a lifetime to grow. It is also of some importance that the top and bottom of the piece are correctly marked or noted since if it is planted upside down the roots will emerge from the "top".

These pieces are selected for shape — the more gnarled and twisted they appear, the more valuable they are. They are then planted in ornamental pots for the development of both buds and roots, usually in the warmth of a glasshouse. After about two months, the stock will be active and ready for grafting. Once grafted, the scion is protected with a plastic bag. By the following spring when the union has taken, some fertiliser is applied, and the plant kept well watered. It may spend the whole of the second year in the glasshouse.

It is anticipated that flower will be produced in the third or fourth year. In the meantime, shaping of the branches will be the main object. Standard wiring is applied in late summer to autumn. Once the tree is established, repotting is needed at two to three-year intervals and can be effected at any time that the plant is not growing.

Unfortunately these camellias are not recommended for temperate zones. Here they produce blossom well after the usual flowering season and, on occasions, new shoots conceal the flowers.

CAMPHOR LAUREL
Cinnamomum camphora

A very large evergreen tree with a pote
tial for extremely long life, camph
laurels are indeed amongst Japan's olde
trees.

They are mostly used in inform
and slanting-trunk, twin-trunk and clu
styles. It is very easy to induce mul
trunks in this tree simply by cutting
down hard, even to soil level. Such wo
should be carried out in late winter
spring.

In cold climates, potting should
carried out in spring, while wiring can
applied most of the year except in wint
In temperate zones, growth is possible f
many months which gives a long period f
pruning, but allows potting for much
the year while wiring is limited to la
summer and autumn.

Propagation is done easily by see
The black berry-like fruit collected
autumn may be sown after cleaning.

EDAR, JAPANESE
ryptomeria japonica

 very tall and stately tree, the leaves are
 vl-shaped, about 1.5 cm long, spirally
 ranged and tapering to a blunt point.
 ue branches occur in whorls which, when
ature, are held out horizontally.

Its elegant shape lends itself to the
 rmal upright style, yet on occasions,
 ulti-trunked forms are seen and in-
 uded in bonsai styling. It is not a popular
 bject, but appears in small numbers in
 e pictorial bonsai magazines.

Potting in the cold zones is in late
 ring, in warm zones from autumn to
 ring, and wiring is possible from late
 ring to autumn. Repotting will be
 cessary every two to three years.

Pruning required will be the re-
 oval of the growing tips right through the
 owing season, but not into late autumn.

Propagation is by seed, if it is
 ailable.

CHERRIES, JAPANESE FLOWERING
Prunus serrulata

The well-known flowering cherries include
many cultivars, mostly of Japanese origin.
All are potential bonsai material, being
suitable even for miniature sizes. Miniatures have been recorded as flowering
regularly every year.

Design can include informal,
slanting and semi-cascade styles.

In the temperate climates, potting
can be carried out from autumn right
through winter to spring.

Wiring is applied in late spring and
summer. All the cherries need some
summer protection in the temperate
zones, and no pruning in wintertime as
this may remove the flower buds. Regular
pruning is safe after flowering.

Propagation — the cherries are now easily propagated from cuttings but layering and grafting are also possible. Two species are worth particular mention.

Yoshino Cherry, *Prunus x yedoensis*
Mostly accepted today to be a natural hybrid, this is an outstanding flowering tree. Earlier flowering than most others, with neat foliage. In cold climates it could produce some fruit.

A two-tree setting or a group planting of three could produce a fabulous spring display. For single trees, informal and slanting trunks are well suited to the cherries.

Weeping Cherry, *Prunus subhirtella* "Pendula"
A well-known garden subject. Its weeping habit brings a change in bonsai design to the weeping-branch style. It is a very graceful plant and is ideal also for cascade style and miniature-size bonsai.

Taiwan Cherry, *Prunus campanulata*
A very early-flowering cherry with rosy-red flowers. In warm temperate climates, the first blossom is seen in winter, and is so regular it could be forecast to the day. By

25 July in the southern hemisphere, it wi be approaching full flower, and in m garden, flowers have been recorded a early as June. It is hardy, flowering fron seed in four years, and one of the fe cherries producing fruit in a warn temperate climatic zone. This could we be a future famous bonsai subject. Flowe fruit and foliage, bark colour and textur all are desirable features.

Bonsai styling ranges from forma upright, informal and slanting to twin an multi-trunks.

Repotting is possible many month of the year in the temperate zones. Wirin is applied after fruit ripens. Watch fc wire biting into the wood — this is vigorous grower.

Propagation is by seed, cutting layering and grafting. Seed is collecte from ripe fruit in late spring to earl summer. It is cleaned and sown in mois sphagnum moss or stratified until th following spring, when it can be sown in standard seed-sowing mix. New shoot emerge in late winter and can be pruned i early spring.

CRABAPPLE
Malus

An outstanding spring-flowering and fruiting tree, for which a large range of species and cultivars is available. It is very popular as a bonsai subject and can be designed in informal upright, slanting, and the two cascade styles, as well as twin-trunk and clump styles.

Some protection may be necessary from fruit-eating birds. My trees are attacked every year by one of the local parakeets, the eastern rosella, *Platycercus eximius*, which tears the apples apart simply to eat the seed.

Potting may be carried out in spring or autumn. Wiring is also possible in spring and autumn. In the colder climates where the apples may remain on the tree to early winter, the autumn leaves may be cut off to expose the whole crop of fruit. Regular pruning is carried out in spring.

Propagation is by seed, cutting and grafting. Collect fruit when ripe in late winter — sow or stratify, then sow in spring. Crabapples are usually propagated by grafting from selected species or cultivars. Seedlings which may occur from fruiting trees take some years to flower and may not be identical with the parent. They are useful as understocks for grafting.

CRAPE MYRTLE
Lagerstroemia indica

A natural, informal upright tree with a tendency to produce multiple trunks. Crape myrtle, well known for its summer flower and its attractive smooth bark, also has attractive foliage colour in autumn.

Repotting is recommended twice yearly in early spring and early summer.

For the protection of the bark, wire should be paper-wrapped and applied in spring to summertime.

Propagation by layer, according to the skill and desires of the grower, can produce almost ready-made trees quite quickly, with trunk diameters of up to 20 to 30 cm.

Hinoki cypress.

Repotting will be necessary ever three years. The Japanese repot at an time of the year (there appears to be no re strictions whatever) and none for wiring a well which could suggest it is a hardy tree

Its main use in bonsai styling i formal upright which follows its norma habit. In particular, the branches an branchlets grow in a flattened horizonta manner, which makes it a very attractive looking tree.

Propagation is by cutting for th dwarf varieties and cultivars, by seed fo the species.

Successful growers should recor details of their culture techniques fo future use.

CYPRESS, FALSE OR HINOKI
Chamaecyparis obtusa
A one-time favourite plant for bonsai culture, the hinoki cypress is now rarely seen on the Japanese show bench.

It is a shapely tree with very attract-ive foliage and, like the cypress, has closely pressed scale-like leaves. The name *obtusa* refers to the blunt apex of the leaves. This plant is easy to identify from the others in the genus from the distinc-tive X and Y markings in white on the underside of the twigs.

There are some varieties and cultivars, mostly dwarfs, with others having golden foliage.

Its rise and fall in popularity could be related to its response to pot culture over long periods. Whilst as a garden plant it requires adequate water, especially in the summer, overwatering in containers causes problems. Perhaps if we follow the Japanese suggestion to water-spray the foliage in summer it could overcome the persistent watering of the soil.

OTONEASTER
otoneaster

elected species, mostly of dwarf
aracter, are popular flowering and
uiting bonsai specimens, being of
terest for much of the year and some-
mes as long as nine months. In Japan the
ck cotoneaster, *C. horizontalis*, is one of
e favourites. In some zones it may
have as a deciduous tree, losing the
ajor portion of its foliage. The leaves are
nall, about 10-15 mm long, often turning
d in autumn before falling.

Other than formal upright, its use is
tended to almost every style, especially
rge group plantings (multiple plantings),
hich produce a spectacular display of
uit from late summer to early winter. Its
rizontal growth habit should be taken
lvantage of, particularly for the cascade
yles.

Those with grafting skills can use
horizontalis on old plants dug from the
rden as weeping-branch style, something
ry different from that produced by most
owers.

A hardy plant, it will tolerate potting
most every day of the year, but not
ring winters in a cold climate. It will
lerate wiring throughout the year as
ll. It will require repotting every three
ars.

Propagation is by the standard
opagating techniques: seed, cutting and
afting are all possible. Fruit is collected
autumn or early winter, cleaned and
red in a dry place for sowing in spring.

DOGWOOD, JAPANESE
Cornus kousa

A well-known spring-flowering tree, sometimes seen as a bonsai specimen. The dogwood has flowers in both white and pink
which look a little like a single rose. Foliage is heat-tender and may require some
summer protection.

As the branching is more or less
horizontal and is easy enough to train
below the horizontal, the dogwood is often
used as a cascade style. It may also
produce multiple trunks and is well suited
to clump style. As an upright tree, it is
suited for the informal upright style.

Potting will be needed every two to
three years and may be carried out from
autumn to spring. Wiring can be carried
out most of the year, but a watch must be
kept against the wire biting into the new
growth.

Propagation is by cutting or layering
to produce early flowering.

Port Jackson fig.

ELM, CHINESE
Ulmus parvifolia

A large, wide-spreading tree with graceful branching. This elm's small leaves make it a popular bonsai subject. Some dwarf-form cultivars are available, with tiny foliage. The bark is attractive and colourful.

It is versatile, being used for most bonsai styles and sizes. The smaller leaves make it useful for miniature work.

Potting may take place many months of the year except in very cold zones. Some leaves may fall during autumn and winter but it is considered evergreen in some climates. Wiring can be applied in late summer.

Long, vigorous shoots may occur in spring. These can be pruned at will.

Propagation is by seed and cutting. Cuttings are a very easy method when pieces of root are used as the cuttings. Selected shaped root pieces make ideal trunks for miniature bonsai. Hardwood or semi-hardwood cuttings are equally successful when given bottom heat. Seed produces variable results with germination often as low as five per cent.

FIGS
Ficus

A large range of mostly evergreen trees found in the warmer temperate zones to the tropics. They are majestic, giant trees for the larger gardens and parks, and in some parts of the world are used as street trees for shade. What could well be a paradox is that these large trees lend themselves to miniature bonsai, and can be easily grown in a pot 2-3 cm long. The leaves reduce in size to be in proportion with the tiny tree.

They will conform to almost any bonsai style. The vigorous showy root system is particularly ideal for root settings and exposed-root style. Grown from seed, they assume a real tree-like shape in about five years with an expanded base tapering to the top.

In eastern Australia, the Moreton Bay fig, *F. macrophylla*, and the Port Jackson fig, *F. rubiginosa*, were some of the first native trees used for bonsai.

In Europe and North America, figs are usually grown as indoor plants, and there is no reason why bonsai figs cannot be kept indoors or in heated glasshouses.

during the winter months in those climates.

Potting is possible any time the tree is not in active growth.

Wiring should be carried out in summer to autumn.

Propagation — seed, cutting, layering and grafting are all possible.

The interesting roots of some figs make them ideal for root over rock settings.

GINKGO, MAIDENHAIR TREE
Ginkgo biloba

An ancient Chinese deciduous tree, well established in Japan. Two old trees in Tokyo withstood the 1923 earthquake, and are still looking good today.

The usual bonsai style for this tree may be classified as formal upright, yet it is different from any other, being pruned into a very compact arrangement.

Potting may begin with leaf fall and continue to spring in the milder climates. Established trees may require root-pruning only every five years.

Propagation is by seed and grafting. Ripe fruit is regarded as ill-smelling and female trees as seed producers are few and far between outside Japan. Seed is mostly imported for sowing in spring.

Horizontal hawthorn.

HACKBERRY, CHINESE
Celtis sinensis

An attractive tree with smooth bark and somewhat elm-like in appearance.

It is a hardy tree for both warm and cold climates and is used in bonsai work throughout the world for formal and informal upright styles, twin-trunk, clump styles and group plantings.

Potting is required at two to three-year intervals and may take place most of the year in temperate zones and in early spring in the colder climates. Wiring is best carried out in late spring to summer while pruning is restricted to early summer.

Propagation is by seed and cuttings. The fruit is often concealed by foliage but, when plentiful, is easy to locate. It should be harvested when ripe in early winter and sown in spring.

HAWTHORN
Crataegus laevigata

The hawthorns, whether from North America or England, are all quite spectacular as bonsai specimens, having a long, colourful period from early spring flowering to late autumn or early winter fruiting. They also have attractive foliage and bark. The one disadvantage of the hawthorns is their thorns, which are sharp and plentiful.

For bonsai, the hawthorn is a tree of many uses. It can be styled as formal, informal, slanting and clump style specimens, as well as for group plantings and raft style.

The wood matures quickly and soon becomes rigid, thus shaping of the new season's growth should not be neglected. It will be ready for wiring in late summer.

Hawthorns are particularly subject to attack by white wax-scale and caterpillars, both of which can be controlled by spraying.

Propagation from seed is possible but these could need grafting for flower and fruit production. Layering is also a useful method with these plants. Fruit is collected when red and fully ripe. Clean seed and stratify in autumn; germination is slow and may take two years.

English hawthorn.

JACARANDA
Jacaranda mimosifolia

A spring-flowering tree from Brazil which could well be classified as the best blue flower in the world. The jacaranda needs a temperate climate to perform its best, but in such climate it responds well to bonsai culture.

However, the very large compound leaves can be a problem for bonsai. There is some reduction in well-established potted plants but the best method of presenting the jacaranda is as a large bonsai which will accommodate the leaves in better proportion and, of course, produce a much more spectacular flowering bonsai.

Formal and informal upright and slanting-trunk styles are suggested as more natural styles for this tree.

Repotting can be carried out from autumn to spring at intervals of two to three years. Wiring may be done after the main flush of growth has settled down.

Propagation is by seed or by grafting for quicker flowering. The fruit or woody follicle is brown when ripe and should be sown in late spring or early summer.

Sargent's juniper.

JUNIPER
Juniperus

After the pines, perhaps the second-most popular conifer is the juniper, an ever-green tree or shrub, often with thin, flaking bark. There are many dwarf-type garden plants that can be used.

The leaves are of two types, and may be found together on the one plant, or separately on different plants. They are described as: acicular, awl-shaped or needle-shaped, with a stiff sharp point; or scale-like, tiny undeveloped leaves closely clasping the stem. Some authors refer to the short, needle-like leaves as "juvenile foliage", since most seedlings carry this type of leaf and later develop the scale-like leaves. But this does not apply to all junipers and the needle-like leaves may persist through the life of some of the species, or for many years. The common juniper, *J. communis*, is one of those that never produce any scale-like leaves.

Japan's most popular juniper for bonsai culture is *J. chinensis* var. *sargentii*. Some authors have accepted a new name, *J. sargentii*. This is a prostrate-growing bush with ascending branchlets rising very little above the ground, forming a carpet-like mass of foliage. Both types of leaves may be found at any time on mature plants. The awl-like leaves occur in threes, and may measure up to 9 mm long. The

upper surface has two broad bands o white, divided by a very thin green line - not always conspicuous.

This variety has many uses in bonsa design, being very popular for the styl known as driftwood, which displays a ancient gnarled and twisted trunk, a par of which is dead. Exposure to element whitens the dead wood, hence the nam driftwood. Informal, slanting, semi cascade and cascade styles are als popular.

Potting of junipers can be carrie out almost throughout the year, excep winter in the cold areas, and it will b needed every two to three years. Much th same timing is appropriate for the appli cation of wire.

Pruning, once the shape has bee developed, is mostly nipping out the ne buds, leaving a few needles or scale-lik leaves behind. In its early life, care shoul be taken to avoid the needle-sharp point of the acicular leaves which can be ver unpleasant on occasions when one i handling junipers.

Propagation — seed and cuttings ar both possible.

A miniature Sargent's juniper, 19 cm high.

LLYPILLY
mena smithii

n Australian native tree that has
tential for many bonsai styles as it
curs in nature in many different guises
 formal, informal upright, multi-trunk,
ouped and even growing in raft style.

The lillypilly is colourful almost
ar round with handsome grey-green foli-
e, attractive flowers and ornamental
uit, not unlike a cherry in shape, size and
lour. It is evergreen with smooth bark of
ht-brownish colour.

In temperate areas, it is possible to
ot-prune and pot in all seasons. In colder
eas, this is possibly best restricted to
tumn — after fruiting. Some seedlings
re donated to the School of Horticulture
Tokyo, but no comment has been made
 to the tree's acceptance of cold winter
ather.

Wiring can be applied from the end
the accepted growing season.

Pruning can take place in spring and
mmer, but not too late to restrict the
st of the season's growth. However,
tumn growth has been recorded after
avy rain.

Propagation is usually from seed
hough some grafting has been success-
l. Collect fruit when red and fully ripe.
ean off the flesh and sow in late autumn
winter.

LIQUIDAMBAR
Liquidambar styraciflua

A large deciduous tree with maple-like
leaves, but tolerant of much warmer
climates than the maples. It is ideal in
temperate zones where autumn colour can
be achieved with little or no trouble. There
are a number of species available with
some cultivars of superior colour.

In nature the liquidambar has a very
formal habit of growth, and thus formal
upright is the most suitable bonsai style
for this tree, but it will produce multi-
trunks if severely pruned to ground level.

In warm zones, potting can be done
at any time. In colder areas, spring is the
best time. Wiring is applied when seasonal
growth slows down in late summer to
autumn.

Propagation is by seed or grafting
for cultivars. Seed can be stored over
winter in damp sphagnum moss or sown
when collected in late autumn or early
winter.

that seedlings may take up to 25 years to flower, so that propagation from cuttings is a more usual method of propagation. Established garden trees can also be dug up, pruned and potted.

MAGNOLIA
Magnolia — selected species

Magnolias are among the most beautiful of flowering trees and shrubs. The deciduous varieties, which are recommended for bonsai, bloom in early spring and late winter in temperate areas, when their large tulip-like flowers are much admired. Those growers who are under the impression that flowers must be small can rejoice that even the magnolia is an accepted bonsai subject.

Informal upright, slanting, semi-cascade and cascade are suitable styles for a single-trunk magnolia. Twin-trunk and clump styles are also possible.

Magnolias will require repotting every two to three years. They are usually potted on completion of flowering and can be wired from spring to autumn. They will require summer protection in most climates.

Propagation is by seed, cutting or layering. Collect seed when ripe — sow or stratify, then sow in spring. But do note

Many figs have partly exposed roots when growing naturally.
They are thus ideal subjects for the root over rock style.

A coiled style seedling crabapple, *Malus,* displayed indoors.

Japanese maple.

vegetatively propagated from a single, superior parent tree.

Some variation occurs in bark texture and colour as well as shape of foliage.

There must be some discrimination used when selecting maples for rock settings. The trident maple is acknowledged by the Japanese as ideal for this setting because of its showy root system.

Root-pruning and potting will be required every two to three years and is carried out in autumn when the leaves fall. In temperate climates, this can continue through the winter and early spring.

Wiring for shape is begun in summer.

Defoliation may take place in late spring or early summer while normal pruning can be carried out in late winter or early spring and in the early growth period.

Propagation is from seed, cuttings, layering and grafting. Collect seed when ripe in late summer to autumn. Sow it while fresh, or store in moist sphagnum moss. In warm zones, seed can be stratified.

APLES
cer

aples occur mostly as small trees of egular shape, some having straight nks. Most are deciduous and heat- nder and may require some summer otection, particularly in temperate nes.

They lend themselves to a variety of les and sizes but are mostly seen in the formal upright style which most closely sembles their natural shape. However, mal, slanting, semi-cascade and scade styles are possible and maples are o ideal for group plantings. When lecting maples for a group planting, es should be culled in both spring and tumn to obtain some uniformity of iage colour. Alternatively plants can be

A twin-trunk style Japanese maple.

English, European, American and Canadian maples can all be used in bonsai work, but two small-leafed species are worth particular mention.

Japanese Maple, *Acer palmatum*

One of the most popular plants in bonsai, this maple has very attractive leaves, mostly palmate in shape and small enough to suit the smallest miniature-size planting. There is also a range of cultivars with various leaf colours.

Trident Maple, *Acer buergenianum*

A more formal maple with light-coloured bark and foliage which is generally smaller than Japanese maple. The leaves, each with three lobes, give this species its common name. On rare occasions, autumn colour may extend from the yellows to red. This is a native of China and Korea and it is well established in Japan. This species is particularly useful in rock settings where its showy root system is prized.

Informal upright style Japanese maple.

MULBERRY
Morus alba

Another attractive fruiting tree having quite large leaves, even when grown in a pot for some years. It is thus suggested that mulberry be grown as a medium-size or large bonsai, which in turn will give more abundant edible fruit.

Bonsai styling includes informal, slanting, twin-trunk and clump styles and, if the weeping form is available, cascade or weeping-branch style. The weeping form can be easily grafted onto seedlings.

Wiring may be carried out in late spring to summer.

Potting will be required every one to two years and is possible almost any day when the tree is not growing in temperate zones, and in late winter to spring in cold zones.

Pruning should be done in late spring.

Propagation is by seed — collect ripe fruit, clean and sow, usually in late summer. It is also easy to propagate by layering, and fruiting follows quickly.

and will be necessary every two to three years.

Propagation is by seed or grafting for cultivars. Harvest seed in autumn. Seed collected from the ground under the tree will be viable. Sow and place in a warm position. Many will germinate in a week or two.

Pin oak, *Quercus palustris.*

English oak, *Q. robur.*

AKS
Quercus

...any species are usually available, as are a few cultivars, but a particularly ...teresting species is the daimyo oak, *Q. ...ntata.* It has large, ornamental leaves ...t this does not deter the Japanese from ...ing it as a bonsai subject. In Japan the ...ad leaves are allowed to remain through ...nter.

Other oaks have outstanding autumn ...lour, for example the pin oak or marsh ...k, *Q. palustris,* and *Q. coccinea.*

Mature trees do produce fruit ...corns).

The root system of the oaks is ...rhaps of some concern. It has a vigorous ...proot which soon fills the container, ...sulting in the typical coiled or distorted ...rm often seen in potted plants. But, ...spite constant propaganda to the con...ary, *Quercus* roots have proved to be very ...rdy and tolerant of root-pruning.

In its more natural state, most of the ...rger oaks are seen as erect formal trees, ...t on the bonsai show bench may be ...formal, slanting and semi-cascade. With ...vere pruning, twin trunks and multi...unks can be induced.

Trim before the new buds harden. ...ring can be applied through to late ...mmer. Potting may be carried out many ...onths of the year in the warmer climates

OLIVE
Olea europaea var. *communis*
The common olive, mostly a commercial tree, may appeal to the bonsai grower. When seen as a mature tree, its attractive gnarled trunk gives a look of added age which is one of the ideals in bonsai.

    The leaves and branches of olives are of opposite arrangement and will require pruning to produce the alternate arrangement required in all bonsai styles. Informal upright, slanting-trunk and twin-trunk styles are all possible uses for the olive.

    It is a very hardy tree and will tolerate potting many months of the year, repotting being required every two to three years. In cold climates it will need some winter protection. Wire can be positioned from summer to autumn.

    Propagation is by seed. Collect ripe fruit in late autumn or winter, clean and sow at once or stratify and sow in spring.

PEAR, MANCHURIAN
Pyrus ussuriensis
An ornamental flowering pear of some distinction. I often marvel at the perform ance of my garden tree — it flowers perfection and produces the well-know tiny fruit so desirable for miniature bonsa yet its origin is the cold of Manchuria a northern Japan. It tolerates the intens summer heat without even a burnt marg of a leaf.

    Normally an erect tree bons styling can vary from formal, informal a slanting-trunk styles to two-tree setting small groups and raft style, both straig line and sinuous.

    Pruning should be effected aft flowering and wiring applied in late spri or early summer. Potting can be carri out many months of the year when t plant is not in active growth.

    Propagation is by seed, cuttin layering and grafting. For seed, colle ripe fruit, clean and stratify it. Sow spring; seedlings take many years flower.

Black pine, *Pinus thunbergii*.

ERSIMMON
Diospyros kaki

n ornamental fruiting tree with the
dded advantage of good autumn-coloured
oliage. The fruit may be up to 8 cm or
nore in diameter. Such large fruit could
e disproportionate to the miniature plant
ut the imbalance can be dealt with. The
olution is to limit the number of fruit. For
xhibition purposes and also for photogra-
hy, three pieces of fruit are usually
trategically placed to form a triangle,
ith the apex at the top of the tree.

Informal upright is the common
tyle, but also possible are straight-line
nd sinuous raft styles.

As mature wood is brittle, wiring is
arried out from spring through to
utumn. In Japan potting is often done
very year in spring.

Propagation is possible by layering
r grafting.

PINES
Pinus

The Japanese pines are without doubt the
most popular of bonsai subjects.

Bonsai styling of pines is almost
unlimited, but perhaps the most outstanding shape of all is the formal upright.

Pruning is of some importance.
When the new shoots emerge, they are
pinched back, leaving a few bunches of
needles. Additional shoots arising from
this pruning can be treated in the same
way. Branches which have been allowed to
grow can be pruned back to about five
clusters of needles in early autumn. This
is not done every year but every two years,
and produces dense clusters of leaf-
bundles, creating a very natural pine-tree
look. Cones are not used in ornamental
display and it is unimportant if they fail to
develop.

Potting is carried out every two to
three years in spring or autumn, with
wiring applied from autumn through to
winter.

All the pines are sensitive to
overwatering.

Propagation is by seed. In those countries where these trees are not normally grown or not established, seed can be imported (check import regulations). Sow seed in spring.

Three species are worth particular mention.

Japanese White Pine, *Pinus parviflora*

This is also known as the Japanese five-needle pine and, as the name implies, the needles are in bundles of five, and are slender and curved, to about 7 cm long, the margins finely toothed. This can be tested by running the thumb and finger down the length of the needle from the apex to the base. Lifespan of the needles is from three to four years.

There are over 150 variants of this pine, some of which are the most popular pines used and include dwarf forms popular for miniatures. They have been found to be not very tolerant of warmer temperate climates where the black pine is recommended.

Japanese Black Pine, *Pinus thunbergii*

Leaves in pairs, dark green, rigid, up to about 10 cm long. This is a very hardy tree, especially in warmer zones.

Red Pine of Japan, *Pinus densiflora*

The leaves of this pine are in pairs, slender and soft and a lighter green than the black pine. The needles are twisted and the bark is reddish. Though the red pine has been recorded as the most common tree in Japan, it is not as popular as the other two in bonsai work.

QUINCE, FLOWERING
Chaenomeles speciosa

A very hardy deciduous shrub which heralds the spring with its early flowering in some areas even flowering in winter. I has one disadvantage — its needle-sharp thorns, which make it a pruning hazard. Its long-standing common name, japonica, misleads the gardening fraternity as to its origin. It is a Chinese plant. The flowers are roundish in shape and they appear before the leaves with an abundance rarely seen, in colours of white, pink, red and two tone colours. Single-flower forms are usually selected for bonsai.

Many bonsai styles are possible, but most often seen is a multi-trunk setting (clump style), which produces a massed flower effect.

Pruning, done after flowering to control shape and size, will in turn develop more shoots from the base. Most of these or all of them must be removed to control the number of trunks. The new shoots on the trunk or branches are allowed to develop five to seven nodes before pruning. Wire at any time, but watch the thorns.

Potting is usually carried out at intervals of about three years. It can be done almost at any time, except in spring or autumn in the cold areas.

This plant is subject to attack by white wax-scale which can be kept under control by spraying.

Propagation — this is one of the easiest plants in the world to propagate by the use of root cuttings. These can be collected at the time of repotting or taken from a garden plant. The length of cuttings should be 5-10 cm or more, and they may be shallow-planted in a horizontal position or may be planted vertically, as are standard cuttings.

Rhododendron serpyllifolium.

RHODODENDRON AND AZALEA
Rhododendron and *Azalea*

The genus *Rhododendron* is perhaps better known for its contribution to azalea bonsai, although most of the genus can be used. Like camellias, these are grown specifically as flowering bonsai and, as such, are subject to some of the same rules; once again, single flowers are selected.

Azalea bonsai

A large range of species, hybrids and cultivars is generally available in countries where azaleas are popular as garden plants. Many countries have developed their own special types, some of which may have limited seasons for flower. Others may flower intermittently for many months of the year. For exhibition purposes, it may be desirable to choose the main range of bonsai azaleas with similar flowering habits.

In Japan, for example, the most popular is the *satsuki* (a May flower), which has single flowers and produces one flower per bud. *Satsuki* bonsai are formed most frequently in the style of an aged pine tree and there are two major methods of achieving this. One is to use an aged

An 80-year-old *satsuki* azalea.

Rhododendron lochae.

satsuki taken from its natural environment or a garden and shape this into bonsai. The other is to use a two- or three-year-old tree and, by the use of wires, shape it into bonsai. By the time the young *satsuki* is five years old, it will begin to have good form, and at about 10 years, with the increased size in its trunk it will be well shaped as a bonsai.

Bonsai styling for azaleas and rhododendrons can be formal or informal upright, slanting, semi- and full cascade styles, twin-trunk and clump styles, straight-line and sinuous raft, exposed-root style, rock settings and group plantings. A large range from which to select your favourite shape.

The grouping of azaleas is becoming very complex today. Europe, America, Australia and New Zealand are all developing their own particular cultivars to suit climatic requirements.

The broad-leafed rhododendrons are rarely seen, yet these in turn are equally hardy and the more courageous bonsai grower can include them in his or her collection. After many years' work in my part of the world, not acknowledged as rhododendron country, selected broad-leafed rhododendrons are well established and are equal to any other flowering plant used for bonsai.

Australia's only representative of the genus, *Rhododendron lochae*, of tropical origin from Cape York Peninsula, now classified under the vireya rhododendrons, was used early in the work together with some of the first hybrids. They proved superior bonsai subjects.

Azaleas and rhododendrons will require repotting every one to three years. This is carried out in late summer to the following spring — spring itself being the only unsuitable season for this work.

Propagation is mostly by semi-hardwood cuttings taken in early summer, or by grafting on selected understocks grown from seed. Propagation from seed is also possible. Seedlings take some years to flower, and need not be the same as the parent plant — harvest the capsules when ripe, and keep dry and warm to encourage splitting of the capsules; sow in spring.

Propagation is mostly by seed which is freely available on mature trees. Cones are harvested when fully ripe in early winter and stored in a warm place for discharge of seed. Sowing is in spring when temperatures are warm and stable. Semi-hardwood cuttings have also been successful.

IE-OAK
asuarina cunninghamiana

a attractive Australian conifer-like tree nich was freely used by the Japanese sidents of Hawaii as a bonsai subject ng before bonsai culture was introduced to Australia.

The foliage is reduced to mere ales, with the branchlets having the pearance of needle-like leaves. To add its pine-like appearance, it produces a oody cone. It has been suggested that its nilarity to a pine tree is the reason for popularity with the Japanese Hawaiians no have had particular success with a tural dwarf form in miniature work.

Casuarina cunninghamiana is mostly uined into a formal upright style and ring can be carried out from late mmer. Potting is possible in autumn d spring and will be necessary every two three years. Pruning is carried out in ring to summer.

Norway spruce.

SPRUCE
Picea

An evergreen tree that is widespread in the northern hemisphere, and introduced into the southern hemisphere, being well known in Australia and New Zealand in selected climatic zones. The trees are pyramidal in shape and are thus perfect for bonsai. There are many cultivars of dwarf character, ideal for rock settings and miniature work. With the common spruce, *P. abies*, the branches are nicely spread, the needle-like leaves short and well in proportion, and persistent for three or four years.

In Japan such trees as the black spruce, black ezo spruce, *P. jezoensis*, and the common ezo spruce, *P. glehnii*, and cultivars, are traditional bonsai material, but are said to be sensitive to big-city pollution and rarely appear in the bonsai nurseries.

Bonsai styling, first and foremost, is the beautiful formal upright tree, coiled and split-trunk, driftwood style representing aged trees, exposed-root and root over rock styles.

Pruning or trimming is carried out in spring, the new shoots are allowed to elongate, then are cut or pinched back, allowing a few needles to remain at the base. This in fact stops all growth for that year and is often disappointing to the bonsai newcomers. The effect is t produce more buds for the next year an thus make the tree in training mor compact.

Potting may be done in spring o early autumn and will be required ever two to three years. In the warme climates, keep repotted plants in shad for some weeks. Wiring can be carried ou from autumn to winter.

Propagation is by seed, cutting (thi is essential for the reproduction of th dwarf cultivars) and grafting. Seed, wher available, is sown in spring.

A group setting of Norway spruce.

Allow the long pendulous shoots to grow, pruning back when repotting or in late summer. On occasions, this tree is repotted twice a year from early spring to summer.

Propagation is very easy from cuttings.

LLOW, WEEPING
lix babylonica

graceful tree with pendulous branches, ually seen in the vicinity of water. Of inese origin, its weeping form appeals western bonsai growers, but it is rarely en in Japan. In warm temperate zones, it quick to show its dislike of the hot ather, wilting daily at the first breath of mmer, with leaf-burning followed by foliation later in the season. Summer re can include keeping the willow bonsai a water basin.

It has been suggested that the eping willow can be used as a rock tting as well as the obvious weeping-anch style.

WISTERIA
Wisteria (Wistaria)

A most spectacular flowering vine. It is specified as a flowering plant when used in bonsai and it is rarely seen at any other time of the year.

The Japanese wisteria, *W. floribunda*, and the Chinese wisteria, *W. sinensis*, are both popular. To distinguish between the two, count the number of leaflets on the compound leaves. The former have 11 to 15 and the Chinese have nine to 13.

A less vigorous-growing form under the Japanese name of *issai* may be available. It is sometimes listed as a dwarf form. The most outstanding form has an inflorescence almost 1 m long and has been exported to most parts of the world, under its Japanese name of *kyashaku*. This form flowers about two weeks after other wisteria.

Flower colours vary from purple, blue, white and pink, and a double-flow form exists.

For bonsai styling, wisteria's use limited to informal upright, slanting ar coiled style, semi- and full cascade whic allow full exposure of the elongate inflorescence.

Potting usually takes place aft flowering; in the warmer zones, from lea fall to spring, and will be necessary eve year.

Wiring and shaping can be carrie out from spring to summer.

Pruning during the growing seasc entails repeated pinching out of the ne shoots, leaving behind two or three buds encourage growth, which will increas flower bud. Long shoots allowed to gro during the summer should all be cut bac at the end of the growing season or winter. All the dead flowering stalks ar removed.

Because of the vigorous summe growth, the Japanese sometimes kee wisteria in a water basin throughout th season.

In Japanese gardens, wisteria usually trained into tree shapes. Stake and specially designed frames are ofte used to assist in shaping.

Propagation is by layering, e pecially where a branch comes into conta with the soil — a very natural sequence events. Garden plants of any age can l dug out, pruned and potted. Wisteria m: also be grown by seed, and this wou probably flower in about five years more.

Australian Native Trees

The value of Australian native trees for bonsai is still to be fully appreciated. The Moreton Bay and the Port Jackson figs, trees which in nature grow as big as any oak tree, have proved to be hardy, easy to handle and easy to train into formal and informal styles and exposed-root and rock settings. Most remarkable is their adaptability to miniature work. It is quite remarkable to see these erstwhile giants reduced to a few centimetres, growing successfully in a pot with only a teaspoon of soil.

Other Australian trees that have been trained successfully include the Illawarra flame-tree (*Brachychiton acerifolius*), Queensland bottle tree (*Brachychiton rupestris*), banksia (*Banksia serrata*), bottlebrush (*Callistemon citrinus*), blueberry ash (*Elaeocarpus reticulatus*), a number of eucalypt species and *Rhododendron lochae*. It was found that these plants could be treated in exactly the same way as any other tree being prepared and cared for in bonsai work.

ELKOVA, JAPANESE
elkova serrata

large deciduous tree related to the elms, ving a distinctive branch arrangement om which a particular bonsai shape own as broom style is evolved. This kes its name from the old-fashioned ooms made of twigs of birch and other es, tied tightly and fixed on a larger anch (the handle).

It is a traditional and popular bonsai bject, and may be seen in a root over ck style, group planting and, on rare casions, as an informal tree.

Wiring can be applied most of the ar. Potting should be carried out every o to three years in spring in the colder nes, and many months of the year in the armer parts of the world.

Pruning to maintain the distinctive oom shape will be needed in spring to te summer.

Propagation is from seed, cutting d layering. Seed harvested in autumn ien ripe is stratified, then sown in spring.

BIBLIOGRAPHY

Yoshimura, Yuji and Halford, Giovanna M., *The Japanese Art of Miniature Trees and Landscapes,* Charles E. Tuttle Co., Tokyo, Japan, 1960.

Kawamoto, Toshio and Kurihara, Joseph Y., *Bonsai — Saikei,* first limited edition, Nippon Saikei Co., Tokyo, Japan, 1963.

McKeown, Keith C., *Australian Insects,* Royal Zoological Society of New South Wales, Sydney, Australia, 1945.

Naka, John Yoshio, *Bonsai Techniques,* Bonsai Institute of California, Santa Monica, USA, 1973.

Rowell, Raymond J., *Ornamental Flowering Trees in Australia,* A. H. & A. W. Reed Pty Ltd, Sydney, Australia, 1980.

INDEX